# Shock Therapy
# and Privatization
## An Analysis of Romania's
## Economic Reform

**DAN GRINDEA**

EAST EUROPEAN MONOGRAPHS, BOULDER
DISTRIBUTED BY COLUMBIA UNIVERSITY PRESS, NEW YORK
1997

# EAST EUROPEAN MONOGRAPHS, NO. CDLXXIX

# CONTENTS

# FOREWORD

This book represents the first part of a research on transition and reform in Romania and how to accelerate the privatization process.

Chapter I refers to a number of theoretical issues that need to be clarified in order to proceed with the analysis; Chapter II explains the reasons for the failure of shock therapy in a number of ex-communist countries, not so much due to existing subjective conditions (though these cannot be totally ignored), but mainly due to the absence of some objective pre-conditions necessary for its successful implementation. The thesis of a "mixed therapy" is presented in this context as a viable alternative for the above-mentioned countries. In Chapter III the author subjects to criticism the way in which reform has been implemented, especially because of the economic disequilibrium which was created after price liberalization due to the absence of a privatized economy, the lack of a competitive market and an insufficiently defined private sector.

Chapter IV tackles the basic problems of the acceleration of privatization. It mainly stresses the need to transform as quickly as possible the nature of some state institutions (with a key role today) and to overview some existing legislation in order to speed the growth of the private sector. In this context special attention is paid to the Private Ownership Fund (POF) which should have a very complex role in the future. Another important issue is the one of the Certificates of Ownership (CO) or vouchers. Some years ago, the author has expressed his doubts with regard to these Certificates but as this idea has now been implemented, he would like to suggest some ways to convert these Certificates into real financial instruments.

Chapter V, the final chapter of the book, underlines the thesis that the success in this transition period in Romania (and perhaps in other ex-communist countries) is extremely dependent on agriculture which, under the above-mentioned circumstances, should become temporarily the engine of economic development and should have a priority position in the entire economy. Clearly, the main course to achieve this is to restructure the state budget and to direct its "eyes" towards the countryside. For these reasons, the author refers only tangentially to industry in this book, stressing its leading role in the future after its technological modernization. Of course, the author sees the agriculture of which he is speaking about in the context of the contemporary scientific revolution (in equipment, technology, and the new achievements in agri-biology, etc.) and taking into account the financial economic incentives existing for agricultural producers in a free market economy. Further, in order to insure the transparency needed in the process of privatization, the author proposes a new budgetary scheme emphasizing the importance of a proper taxation policy for creating a middle class as a basic pre-requisite for a free market economy.

Finally, this chapter ends with the issue of the social safety net, the importance of which was strongly underestimated in this transi-tion period. Because of that, the results of the economic reform were severely negatively affected. Various ways to finance this process are presented in Chapter V.

The efficiency of the privatization program of the Romanian government, proposed in June 1994 (and eventually enacted into law in the second part of 1995 after many postponements) is raising, in the author's view, many question marks. As it will be seen later in this work, it may also build a climate favorable to a rapid growth of inflation mainly because of the lack of a secondary capital market which is only in a gestation phase. Aside from these shortcomings, the law regarding the privatization program does not define priori-ties needed for the economic strategy, nor the need for strengthening the social safety net.

The acceleration of privatization is not only possible but imperative for all ex-communist countries in order to build a free market economy. Of course, everything depends on how this very complex and important process is going to be conceived, what will be its main directions, and what methods will be used for its imple-mentation.

As the privatization programs in other former communist countries are similar in many respects to the one which is being examined here, the author believes that some of the proposals put forward in this book may have a wider geographical applicability – taking, of course, into consideration the specific local conditions.

The model that is presented in this study could also be useful for other small or medium sized countries which are contemplating dismantling their centralized planned economies, such as some African or Asian countries.

The first version of the book was published in the Romanian language in 1994. Although the present English version includes an important part from the first version, there are also significant changes, starting with the title of the book. Also there are some new paragraphs and some chapters of the book are extended in order to give a better understanding for the Western reader.

The author thanks all those who helped with the English version of the text, and especially the Republic National Bank of New York for its financial assistance. Needless to say, the author assumes full responsibility for the ideas expressed in this book.

Regretfully, we lack the information as to whether some proposals or ideas advanced in the book have already been or are presently being implemented in Romania.

Dan Grindea

# INTRODUCTION

A new historical event is deemed to have taken place when "something" of an overwhelming proportion occurs. Although not totally unexpected, this event, due to its magnitude and ramifications, takes the world by surprise and leaves it breathless for a while.

Such was the case in 1789 when the French Revolution began; in 1917, with the onset of the Russian Revolution, or in 1989 with the collapse of the communist empire in Eastern Europe, followed by the disintegration of the Soviet Union.

In historical terms, the so-called "era of communism" was the shortest compared to those of feudalism and capitalism. Its short-lived existence was a direct result of the circumstances under which it emerged. It came about not as a natural process led by existing objective socio-economic and political conditions, but as a process imposed by subjective forces at the beginning of the twentieth century.

The people who lived through this apocalyptic experience are now trying very hard to find a way out from an ultra-centralized system to a free market economy. In order to have a proper perspective on the transition process, one must clearly understand the events that occurred in 1917, which made possible such a "historical accident" in this part of the world.

It is not the purpose of this book to dwell on the obsolete nature of certain Marxist propositions which were viewed as sacred by some people some several decades ago. The history of this century has proved in an indisputable way that some fundamental premises of Marxist ideology have been invalidated, step by step, by modern technological achievements. The amplitude of the technological revolution which is taking place in front of our eyes has greatly affected the nature of the economic relations in the process of production by introducing new elements that could not have been imagined a century ago like the powerful role of trade unions, or the enormous impact of the social protection programs in the areas of education and health care, etc.

At almost one hundred and fifty years after the publication of the "Communist Manifesto," the utopian nature of the Marxist solution and the deplorable results of its implementation are obvious (even though Marxism is still fashionable in some under-developed

1

countries). This fact, regretfully, did not prevent some remarkable scientists and cultural personalities, as well as other people of high moral standing, from being sincerely attracted to this doctrine in their search for human progress and from being ready to sacrifice themselves for this utopia.

As the regretful political scientist Raymond Aron wrote, Marxism became a kind of "opium for the intellectuals." This "opium" had such a powerful effect that even those criticizing Marxism did not notice a flagrant contradiction between the theoretical and the practical evolutionary stance of Marx. In this respect his well-known 1848 slogan, "Proletarians of all countries unite" (for the socialist revolution), irrespective of the developmental level of their countries, was totally in conflict with his thesis, formulated twenty-five years later in the "Critique of the Gotha Program" (1872), according to which the socialist revolution could only succeed in the highly developed industrial countries. Could it be that Marx himself was not aware of this contradiction or that he did not desire to correct it? And, even if he had corrected this slogan, could it have changed Lenin's thoughts on the matter?

In retrospect, it is now much clearer that Lenin, relying on only a very short period (the first one and a half decades of this century), disrupted and distorted by the First World War and under the influence of the disastrous situation in tsarist Russia, decided that it was time to "update" Marxist theory on the socialist revolution.

The facts analyzed by Lenin – despite their limited relevance in both geographic and economic terms – were extrapolated by him to the entire capitalist world (see especially his "Imperialism, the Highest Stage of Capitalism," written in 1916 and "The State and the Revolution," published in 1917). From this analysis he drew the following conclusions which became the "Bible" for his revolutionary movement: a) the capitalist system is moribund and is ready for revolutionary change; b) this revolution should start not in the advanced industrial countries (as Marx had taught him) but in the under-developed ones, where the capitalist chain is weaker; c) the front-runner of this revolution should be the proletarian class (regardless of its lack of education and political experience), under the leadership of its Communist Party.

After 1917, because of the lack of economic, social and political circumstances that could lead to such a revolution, Lenin's criticism of the capitalist system became, paradoxically, the characteristic feature of his so-called "socialist revolution." However, in contrast to capitalist development, his system was framed with many barriers, which have now, in turn, become the main obstacles to the transition to a free market economy.

Indeed, proletarian dictatorship, which was intended to create a mass political democracy, became a strictly personal dictatorship. Socialist property, which was to be owned by workers in order to abolish once and for all the process of exploitation of man by man, became state property– in fact, the property of a very small group, whose "power" was out of the control of the population. In this way there were no limits to the exploitation of the masses. A monopolistic, centralized economy, considered unacceptable even under capitalism, was substituted for economic competition. It was not surprising that under these circumstances the matter of personal freedom was totally ignored.

Lenin's impatience to start his socialist revolution gave him an easy victory in the short term (tsarism collapsed for a many other reasons), but caused long-term disaster, not only for the Russian people but also for the peoples of many other countries (especially in neighboring Eastern Europe and Asia). It also led to many social and political upheavals all over the world. The only "positive" conclusions which can be drawn (if one can accept them as positive) are:

a) the catastrophic outcomes of the existing system in the former Soviet Union (although very little of these had actually been known in the 30s and 40s) were sufficient for the people in the West to have reasonable suspicions about Lenin's experiment. Who knows what would have happened to the rest of mankind if the Russian revolution had not occurred in 1917 but during the Depression years of the 30s when the West was going through a deep economic crisis and was ready for a social upheaval (which, as we know, found its extreme forms in Germany, Italy, and so on?)*

---

* President F.D. Roosevelt deserves special credit for the implementation of "The New Deal," which in fact significantly corrected the disequilibrium in the relations of production, brought to an end the long-lasting economic depression, and also decreased the influence of the former Soviet Union on the "American Left."

b) The total failure of the satellites of the former Soviet Union in Eastern Europe and in Central Europe after the Second World War destroyed the credibility of the Soviet Communist system for the rest of the world. The downfall of the Soviet empire in 1991, which began in 1989 with the disintegration of its satellites in Central and Eastern Europe, took place very quickly due to the deep, though carefully hidden, political, economic and social erosion within it. It was Gorbachev who, of course, unintentionally facilitated the acceleration of this downfall by his domestic and foreign policy. A correct evaluation of the consequences of this policy helped some researchers to form a prognosis of the coming events.*

To change the political structure is a very difficult task for the progressive forces; but to change the economy is much more difficult, as the disastrous inheritance from the Soviet communist system in the field of monetary reform, nationalization and collectivization must be done away with. All of these had been implemented by force.

One cannot merely turn the historical clock back even if, paradoxically, the task at hand is to create the political and socio-economic environment that existed in the pre-communist era. It is necessary to formulate democratic economic proposals and to implement them as soon as possible. In this respect, all the East European countries are to be commended for having started to build a legal framework for the transition period and some important legislation has already been enacted. But the difficulties surfaced once these measures were applied regarding the fight against corruption, bureaucracy, the corrections of economic imbalances, aggravated by an extensive "black market," and so on; in short, the goal was to replace the old system with a free market system in which the "invisible hand" referred to by Adam Smith could actually function.

---

* In 1988 I attended the IMF and the World Bank session in West Berlin. I had the opportunity to study the very big financial arrangements that were supposed to be signed between the West German government and Gorbachev and I reached an unexpected conclusion: the reunification of Germany could happen very soon. Of course, when I returned to New York and presented my thoughts in a written report, I was ridiculed. The only person who approved my idea after reading this report was Dr. Henry Kissinger, who commented, "I substantially agree with your analysis." One year later the Berlin Wall collapsed.

The above-mentioned difficulties were exacerbated by both domestic and external conditions. The most important ones are:

a) The previous despotic legislation and, sometimes, after 1989, the advent of disorganized opposition groups tending to work together with communist dissidents or, at times, the direct ascent to power of communist dissidents and their total or partial refusal to cooperate with other political groups. Under both circumstances, but especially under the second scenario, the implementation of reforms, albeit approved by the legislatures in various countries, was very slow to materialize. Sometimes reform was actually stopped in its tracks because, with few exceptions, the old state apparatus had no incentives to enact significant changes;

b) After five decades of strictly following the decisions of the central authorities, there is still a strong feeling of fear, even among those interested in democratic change, to accept or assume risk, which should be an intrinsic part of the management of a private enterprise;

c) After many years of rejecting the idea of private ownership by the communist regime, there is still widespread skepticism as to whether or not the present government is willing to guarantee this kind of property;

d) The prevailing mentality, fed during a long period of centralized economic planning, which denied the role of profit as the main indicator of economic efficiency and the most important motivation for private investors in their activity; therefore it is not a surprise that a businesslike spirit was almost completely nonexistent;

e) A distorted system of economic information used in all these countries, as well as a distorted price system and foreign exchange rates (some corrections were introduced over the last several years). Obviously, under these circumstances, the signals given by the market to economic agents were absent;

f) A distrust in the competence of those selected to head the various economic departments and in their decisiveness in implementing the necessary reforms.

Due to the above-mentioned inheritance from the former regime, it was practically impossible to set up in all these countries a free market system in a relatively short period without a continuous and substantial influx of technical and financial assistance from the West.

Not only were the domestic financial resources existing in these countries in 1990 insufficient for an extensive privatization of their economies, but significant branches of these economies were (and sometimes continue to be) affected by obsolescence, and many of the enterprises were close to bankruptcy. The hesitancy of some foreign investors in taking important financial decisions with regard to their participation in the economic activity of these countries is understandable, at least for the time being. The previously mentioned difficulties are exemplified by the economic situation in the former East Germany, which was unable to tackle these problems without enormous financial assistance from the former West Germany.

Keeping in mind these difficulties, we can now advance a very general outline of the main objectives of any economy that has to undergo the transition from a centralized totalitarian system to a democratic free market one. They are as follows:

1. Political democratization starting with the lower levels up to the top. This means a thorough liberalization of political life and the replacement of the old state apparatus with new free-thinking people who would tackle the dramatic social and economic changes without any preconceived ideas.
2. Privatization and the building of a new economic and social framework capable of attracting domestic and foreign investment by offering real incentives, based on efficiency.
3. The liberalization of labor legislation, commercial activity and of the price, banking, and financial systems and the development of an attractive capital market.
4. A social safety net to protect the unemployed due to the privatization process from the consequences of inflation, etc.
5. A receptive attitude towards market changes and incentives to attract the population to the labor market.
6. Monetary convertibility accompanied by the foreign financial assistance needed for its implementation.

These six objectives are interconnected to such an extent that any attempt to separate any one of them from the others could damage the entire transition process.

The failure of some models for the transition period implemented in some of the former communist countries was, among other causes, due to the belittling of the importance of these interconnections, priorities, of the pace and sequences of this process, or when some of the above-mentioned changes were given more weight than others. The only possible exception could be the introduction of a monetary convertibility which requires the prior implementation of the other five measures. However, during the transition period even monetary convertibility should be introduced step by step by a skillful combination of the economic, financial, and monetary mechanisms on the domestic market as well as in foreign economic relations.

The purpose of this study is to research, without exhaustive intentions, the degree to which the above-mentioned objectives have been properly implemented in Romania and to offer some suggestions for measures which are needed in order to speed up the privatization process.

# I

## ROMANIA'S POLITICAL AND ECONOMIC STRUCTURE AFTER 1989 (APPEARANCES AND REALITY)

Decisions about the transition and reform strategy in Romania, as well as about its pace and sequence require a clear definition of the political and economic structures after the 1989 revolution.

### A. ABOUT THE POLITICAL STRUCTURE

The official stand is that a people's revolution overthrew the communist dictatorship and undertook the creation of a democratic form of government and a free market economy. The abundant information, often incomplete and contradictory, presented in books, articles, and interviews published after 1990 indicates, however, that the revolution was the result of a strange combination of popular forces, especially belonging to the young generation and a relatively small group – let's call it "the old guard," made up of party apparatus (dissatisfied with Ceausescu), security, army, and police leaders, all of whom had a strong capacity to decide, control, and influence the development of events.

The divergent strategic interests of these two unequal groups (both in terms of numbers and power of decision) for carrying through the long-awaited revolution would surface shortly during 1990 in a strong and open conflict.

After the common goal of the liquidation of the Ceausescu clan was reached, the ways of these two groups diverged considerably. Once the sentence against Ceausescu was carried out and he was executed, the representatives of the young generation as well as of some political parties banned under communism plus some independent-democratic organizations who viewed the liquidation of the dictator as being the only way to a radical change of the existing totalitarian system, felt extremely frustrated because they were unable to reach their goal. They vehemently denied the legitimacy of the new government, referring to a dangerous "conspiracy" which had "stolen" the revolution from those who had really carried it out. The representatives of the other group, who viewed the liquidation of the dictatorship as a way to implement a number of rather limited reforms within the same socio-political system (though not admitting to this publicly), were continuously stressing their crucial contribution to the success of the revolution and especially the support they enjoyed from the population in the 1990 and 1992 elections.

Notwithstanding the desires of these groups, the bizarre circumstances of the revolutionary process in Romania, as well as the unexpected results of the 1990 and 1992 elections after four decades of communist dictatorship, proved that a substantial part of the Romanian people was not prepared for significant changes and preferred to support that political group which was ready to implement only limited economic reforms.

It is thus not surprising to find out from the press and from opposition speeches in Parliament that not only no firm measures were taken to get rid of the bureaucracy left over from the time of the Ceausescu dictatorship, but that important representatives of the power structure of that time continue to be part of this structure. The old way of thinking, incompatible with democracy, is prevalent and the separation of the executive, legislative, and judicial centers of power continue to be unacceptably affected.

In a reference to Romania, an analysis of the situation in the East European countries published by the *Financial Times* on January 24, 1990, starts with the following sentence: "If there is any of the East European countries which will experience most difficulty restoring political institutions and stability, it will be Romania." Four years later we can consider that, with the exception of Yugoslavia, this evaluation was correct.

*Past and present attempts at improving the system*

Regarding the political structure, it is well known that in the past there have been various attempts at improving the "socialist" system. Thus, Stalin thought that by physically liquidating masses of innocent people in the name of salvation of the socialist regime, he was "improving" the system. Khrushchev, unveiling Stalin's criminal actions but leaving untouched the roots of the system, also hoped to "improve" it. History speaks for itself. Perhaps the only attempt at improvement that merits mention here is the "Prague Spring" which occurred more than a quarter of a century ago. The then-Czech president Dubček had come up with the thesis of a "socialism with a human face" as a higher step in the development of the system. Two decades later, Gorbachev returned to the same theme, introducing the ideas of *glasnost* (transparency) and *perestroika* (economic restructuring). Compared to the destructive Stalinist system (which continued its existence for three decades after his death), these ideas were undoubtedly a great improvement. The very point of reference for this comparison, however, namely the Stalinist dictatorial thinking and its tyrannical implementation, are completely unacceptable in this century.

With all their good intentions, neither Dubček nor Gorbachev were capable of realizing that the solution could not be a change in the *policy* of the system but of the *very system* itself. When the Pandora's box was opened in the former Soviet Union, all the pillars on which the system was built started shaking and a few years later the entire system collapsed.

Without diminishing in any way Dubček's good intentions and great courage, in the light of the events of the last decade in the former Soviet Union where Gorbachev's experiment was applied, it is obvious that even if Brezhnev had allowed the Czech leader to complete his experiment, the result would have been the same sooner or later. The failure was caused by the very nature of the so-called "socialist" system. Regretfully this fact was understood very late.

Many honest people from this geographical area acquired this insight belatedly not only due to the misinformation they were the target of, but also because for a decade or more before the revolutions of 1989 there had been some timid attempts at "economic liberalization" in some of the former communist countries of Central and Eastern Europe. These attempts were viewed by naive optimists as a good beginning for improvement, when in fact the basic pillars of the system remained unchanged.

The so-called theory of the "socialist market economy" was elaborated at that time. It has its followers to this day and it is interested in maintaining the same political structure. The peculiar thing about the promoters of this "theory" is their attempt to introduce into the socialist system some functions and mechanisms which are not only utterly strange, but even adverse to it. Thus it is hard to know when misinterpretation ends and where ignorance begins (assuming that good faith exists).

Those who have read Marx's polemical work against Proudhon, "La Misere de la philosophie," cannot ignore the similarity between the above-mentioned "market socialism" and Proudhon's theory about "the market" and "administrative prices" ridiculed by Marx because the intrinsic contradiction between "socialist owner-ship" (as he understood it) and the existence of a competitive market. And if today Marx can be rightly accused for the tragic consequences of his utopia, at least in the above case, he cannot be accused of theo-retical inconsistency. Thus, when we seriously refer to a "market" in the definition given to it by the classics of political economy, from which Marx (as mentioned in his correspondence with Engels) drew many ideas up to a point – after which his thoughts evolved in another direction. This market can be conceived to exist only in an economic democracy, and not within the rigid framework of a so-called "socialism."*

We wish to stress again that either the proponents of the "socialist market" economy are not clear in their own minds as to what they mean when they bring together these two concepts, or they are doing this in order to distort reality for their own political purposes, just as the Russian ultra-nationalist Zhirinovsky refers to his political organization as the Liberal Democratic Party. The fact is that the type of socialism that existed in the former Soviet Union could not coexist with a free market; one or the other must dis-appear.

A new thesis recently in use referring to political structure is that of a so-called "social market economy" which is designed to underline the direction in which Romania should go. Here we also have a strange association of terms. It is well known that when we refer to "the economy" we have in mind "economic activity," or more precisely, the operation of millions of economic agents in their different roles within the production, circulation, distribution, and consumption processes of goods and services in a society. Thus, "the economy" cannot exist in a vacuum, but only within existing society,

---

* A study published in September 1993 by the European Bank for Reconstruction and Development (*The Annual Economic Outlook*, p. 130) mentions that the well-known Polish economist Oskar Lange was writing towards the end of the third decade of this century (when he was a proponent of market socialism) that under socialism, if the enterprises are decentralized, their leaders would compete with each other to obtain capital and labor, attempting to be as efficient as in a capitalist market. Experience has shown, however, that it is not possible to have true decen-tralization in a system in which a party retains the monopoly of power and that it is also idealistic to think that the leaders of the socialist enterprises could be completely devoted to their enterprises instead of to their personal well-being and careers.

be it a more rudimentary or a more advanced society. The economy is *intrinsically* social. To add this word is a truism.

It is, of course, necessary to include the fulfillment of social needs and the degree of their priorities in the political and economic system that is being built, but this very important requirement will not be met by a simple change in labeling. The fact that this name was given to their reform programs by some of the neighboring ex-communist countries cannot justify its use. Every government has the duty to achieve the best combination of economic competition and social safety net in order to protect its citizens against the negative effects of an accelerated privatization, especially during the transition period.

Before concluding these remarks on the political structure, I must refer to an idea that has been put forward for some time in books and articles, namely that in Eastern Europe the entire "transition process" requires a more authoritarian political regime. The recommended model is one of the four "Pacific Tigers" – South Korea, Hong Kong, Singapore, and Taiwan. This idea could be rejected outright. There are perhaps many more authoritarian countries in the world today than democratic ones and on the whole their performance is not superior to that of democracies, quite the contrary. The "Four Tigers" have had, indeed, remarkable economic achievements, but the explanation for their successes should be found in another direction. As opposed to Romania, for instance, these countries never had any form of state monopoly such as "socialist ownership." They did not eliminate private property, nor did they institute "socialist planning." Instead they had a free competitive market and a considerable influx of foreign capital, which came in with no fear of the local political system. The authoritarian regimes were not set up in these countries in order to create a free domestic market, but out of fear of the expansionist tendencies of some of their neighboring "communist" countries, including – five years ago – the Soviet Union. After close to half a century of harsh dictatorship, in Romania an authoritarian regime would only exacerbate the already existing difficulties and would increase the fears of potential foreign investors.

The political profile of Romania, described earlier, was in fact reflected in her economic policies. It has led to specific features in her economic development and was probably the main reason for the unsatisfactory economic performance of the last few years.

## B. ABOUT THE ECONOMIC STRUCTURE

The existing controversies regarding the nature of political power in Romania are matched by those regarding the nature of its economic structure at the time of the 1989 revolution. In this respect it is important to analyze a thesis put forth by Professor Brucan in his book, *Wasted Generation* (Bucharest, 1992).* He states that Romania is changing "from an undeveloped socialism to an undeveloped capitalism." During Ceausescu's dictatorship there was a joke about his slogan, "multilateral developed socialism," by replacing with the "multilateral retarded socialism." But to be serious, this thesis was totally unacceptable for the entire former "socialist bloc," from the river Oder to Vladivostok. A socialist system never actually existed across this immense geographical area, be it undeveloped or somewhat developed. (Of course, the author can be rightly accused that more than two decades ago he himself wrote such aberrations. But that was the "price" which, at that time, everyone was obliged to pay, one way or another, in order to survive.)† In fact, this so-called "socialism" was often qualified in the Western socio-economic studies and, secretly, even in the countries of the "socialist bloc," as a kind of neo-enslavement or neo-feudalism. Attesting to the partial veracity of this observation, sequels of such behavior are still present in the mentality of, and various actions taken by, decision-makers in Romania, substantially complicating the problems of transition.

---

* Professor Brucan's autobiographical book spans a historical period full of surprises retroactively discovered and of profound convulsions with unforeseeable consequences. I read the book with great interest, bearing in mind that in any book of memoirs the author's objectivity and credibility are disputable, and that for a variety of reasons some facts usually remain unwritten. However, the author's efforts to convince us are remarkable. In addition, the courage he portrayed in some earlier works, as well as in Romania's political life between 1987 and 1989, are noteworthy. All these qualify him as a personality that deserves great respect regardless of his ideological background.

† In addition, for me it was the only possible way to publish research showing, indirectly, the complete inefficiency of the socialist "system." As an example, I can mention the book which I wrote in 1958, along with two other authors. The subject was the economic management of industrial enterprises. (I will refer to it briefly in Chapter III.) The book was never distributed to the bookstores because it was banned by the Central Committee of the Communist Party. Another example was my analysis published in 1963 on the correlation between the rate of growth of the total social product (a kind of GNP in the Soviet statistic) and national income in order to prove, in an indirect way, the lack of efficiency of the "socialist" economy, or my criticism in computing the national income, and so forth.

It gradually became obvious that "socialism" was just an "ideological label" camouflaging a very primitive and particularly greedy and destructive <u>monopolistic state capitalism</u> (different, of course, than the one defined by Lenin), endowed with oligarchic tendencies, if we remember the dictator's clan together with his acolytes. Monopolistic State Capitalism (MSC) in socio-economic terms does not necessarily imply high technological progress, financial capital or colonial expansion. In our view, <u>MSC supposes a forced takeover of the national wealth in an overwhelming proportion by the state, namely a leading clique which arbitrarily assumed power and which, through totalitarian policies, was able to dictate the terms of production and consumption of that society, replacing the market economy by a set of centralized administrative measures of distribution</u>. As a result, monetary instruments such as money supply, interest rates, credit, profit, etc., became mere bookkeeping tools without any economic meaning whatsoever. It is therefore not surprising that profitability, one of the fundamental categories of a market economy, became totally irrelevant.

It is a historic irony that this politically abortive regime, which through military force terrorized mankind for almost half a century, and was committed to destroy the MSC in fact – due to the absence of any democratic structure – *embraced* the MSC, with all its negative features, unacceptable in any of the Western countries. (As it is known, the West, in addition to a comprehensive anti-trust legislation, benefits from – and this is truly remarkable – deeply rooted anti-monopoly feelings, without which competition would be inconceivable.)

Therefore the transition of which Professor Brucan is writing is not one from an "undeveloped socialism to an undeveloped capitalism," but rather one from this monopolistic form, euphemistically named "socialist state property," to a pre-monopolistic capitalism. (Underdevelopment in these countries is real but it is not the reason for the above-mentioned problems. I totally agree with Brucan, however, on socialism's incapacity to integrate the new scientific and technological revolution precisely because of its monopolistic structure.)

The practical, albeit unintended, consequences of Professor Brucan's thesis can be identified in certain choices made by Romania's post-communist government in implementing its strategy and its reform program. (We say "unintended" because, paradoxically,

Professor Brucan was forced out of the post-communist political arena.) An example is the government's conceptual framework underlying the privatization plan,* the government's position to "protect" rather than "guarantee" private property (perhaps this has changed in the meantime?), or the various opinions concerning monetary reform as a weapon against inflation,† etc.

A correct understanding of the point of departure on the transition toward a market economy, i.e., a primitive MSC, greatly impacts the kind of decisions needed for this process to succeed. The type of MSC described above is, in our opinion, difficult to match with a shock therapy program, without the presence of certain preconditions. Unfortunately, these preconditions were lacking in most of the East European countries, including the former Soviet Union.

Theoretically one can assume that because the economic system would be the same, this transformation should not encounter special difficulties. However, in practical terms, as was stated previously, the economy consists of an intricate web of relationships and conflicting interests. Those who have brought about "socialist ownership" and have long enjoyed its fruits are not eager to "denationalize" and see it revert to private capitalist ownership. To the contrary, as we will see later in the chapter on privatization, they are desperately striving to become "the new owners of private property." They have the advantage that, due to their past personal relationships, they have access to government institutions (where there were few changes of mentality in executive positions) and to get very good bargains. The absence of real domestic investors (instead of the former nomenclature) and, sadly, the lack of foreign investors has created a very privileged situation for the "new owners." Due to this state of affairs, the old patterns of relationships could still last a long time. For these reasons, the approach and application of shock therapy could not have good results.

It is worth mentioning that the reversal of the process of nationalization has never been an easy one, not even in a traditionally free market, such as that of Great Britain, during Margaret Thatcher's government. However, the economic framework for the conversion was there and de-nationalization, though difficult, was

---

* See the interview given by the author and published in the Romanian newspaper *Libertatea* on July 7, 1991.

† See the author's note published in the newspaper *Romania Libera* on January 22, 1993.

successfully completed. In Eastern Europe, however, where nearly all of the economy has been state-owned, the transition to a market economy is much more complicated. One should also not ignore that in "communist" Romania the former monopolistic state capitalism occurred in the context of a rhetorically anti-capitalist ideology. This fact had a profound negative influence on the way of thinking of the masses, their behavior in various situations, and in their decision-making process.

During a seminar organized by the author of this book (held in Bucharest in November 1990), he extensively referred to the breakup of monopolistic structures and to the creation of a private competitive capitalist sector. In his paper he indirectly criticized the manner in which shock therapy had been applied in Romania and presented the idea of a "mixed therapy" (see the following chapter) as a more efficient alternative. (Unfortunately, the decision-makers in the matter of reform were not present at this seminar.)

Let me conclude these remarks on the economic structure in Romania by quoting Mr. Negritoiu. He was interviewed by *Romania Libera* in January of 1992. Asked where we are witnessing "a revival of economic centralism," he replied:

> We are not witnessing a revival of economic centralism because we never abandoned it.... Economic decentralization by delegation of authority and prerogatives without the right to ownership is an uncompleted form of decentralization. We can only talk of decentralization when the state sector will encompass half of the economy at the most.

At the time of the interview, Mr. Negritoiu was president of the Council for Economic Coordination, Strategy and Reform. Let us only add to his remarks that fifty percent is still a high percentage for the state property in a free market economy.

# II

## THE HAMLETIAN DILEMMA IN IMPLEMENTING THE SHOCK THERAPY NECESSARY FOR A "MIXED THERAPY"

### A. A BRIEF HISTORY OF USING THE SHOCK THERAPY AND ITS OBJECTIVES

The reader of newspapers and of the economic-financial journals, especially those published in the former communist countries of Central and Eastern Europe after 1989, has been simply bombarded day after day with a problem in the form of a dilemma. The problem was whether, in order to effect a smooth transition from a centralized (alleged planned) economy to a free market one, it would be preferable for the governments of those countries to apply a "shock therapy" or a "gradual therapy." This Hamletian dilemma is still awaiting its solution.

Essentially, it was not only a matter of duration, although it is by no means a negligible aspect of the problem, as of the nature of the measures to be taken during this "short" period, measures that would affect the welfare of millions of people in those countries.

Generally speaking, the way in which the problem was presented, it would look as if shock therapy were a specific method for the conversion of the former communist countries to capitalism. Of course, this was not so.

This method was used probably for the first time in 1948 (when the so-called "socialist bloc" was just in the process of formation) in a war-ravaged capitalist country, the former West Germany. The spectacular success of the shock therapy in the rebuilding of post-war West Germany – which according to some commentators occurred "overnight" (not so, of course) – has brought this method to the center of attention. It was viewed as an efficient course of action in countries affected by hyper-inflation due to an excess of cash liquidities, with a budget totally out of balance and with a greatly devalued currency and thus irrelevant in international trade. These circumstances gave rise to a severe scarcity of essential goods for the population, resulting from a catastrophic reduction of the production capacity.

Such situations are typical in countries devastated by war or where dictatorships collapsed under the pressure of the tidal wave of infuriated masses, as happened in the former communist countries of Central and Eastern Europe.

In West Germany, the shock therapy was applied in 1948 as part of a well-thought out plan of monetary reform. It was carefully implemented, and as an essential component of a broad program of economic development. It started with certain shock measures aimed at the control and limitation of money supply in circulation, concurrently with the liberalization of prices for a broad category of goods. Some of agribusiness and a major portion of raw materials remained rationed, both as regards to quantity and prices (textiles and footwear were rationed only as to quantity). In parallel to the considerable reduction of taxes, important measures of social protection were introduced with a view to compensate those affected by the monetary reform. Also, especially in support of the general stabilization program, the non-reimbursable financial aid offered by the Marshall Plan was substantially used.

The recovery process did not proceed as a "triumphal march"; correcting measures were needed until 1953, especially in the financial and monetary sector. It was an outstanding success. In West Germany the recovery went on at a rapid pace; in the European countries that had become satellites of the Soviet empire and where a series of monetary reforms were also implemented between 1946 and 1953, these experiments were, in fact, failures.

The shock therapy has been applied not only in the highly dramatic circumstances outlined above, but also in cases of serious evidence of incompetence in handling state financial resources or some large loans secured through international deals which were used for speculative purpose, or in an irresponsible way at a time when the world-wide market was witnessing unexpectedly great fluctuations of raw materials price, and so forth.

All of the above had devastating consequences for the rate of inflation, unemployment, and the living standards of the masses. In the 1980s a number of Latin American countries found themselves in such a disastrous situation in contrast with what had been ten or twenty years earlier. At that time they had been considered to be quire prosperous. In these cases also, the shock therapy had not been limited to currency reforms, but had been part and parcel of a broad program of economic restructuring.*

The experiment with the shock therapy in West Germany, as well as in some countries of Latin America, seems to lead us to conclude that it may be successfully used in similar circumstances. But let us not hurry to draw this conclusion before looking more attentively at the indispensable conditions in order to achieve success.

Romania's economic circumstances (and they are more or less identical in other former communist states), as well as their social-political consequences, show a great number of similarities with the situations described above which necessitated bringing into operation the shock therapy. Therefore, no one should be surprised that certain international financial organizations (the International Monetary Fund, the World Bank, as well as the European Bank for Reconstruction and Development, etc.) and some prestigious American universities (Harvard, MIT, and others) suggested shock therapy as a solution for shortening the transition period for former communist countries. With this end in view, these institutions have proposed that, in parallel with the democratization of political life, a number of measures be introduced which were drastic compared to the manner in which the economies of these countries were unfolding, such as:

---

\* Incidentally, I should like to mention the fact that, as Chief Economist and Senior Vice-President of the Republic National Bank of New York, I had the opportunity to visit the countries with which the Bank collaborated and to contact personalities from the economic and financial sector as well as politicians. During one such visit to Chile an important politician told me somewhat confidentially that he had some concerns about:

1) the outcome of the general elections to be held soon and which he was hoping could result in bringing to power a government of civilians;

2) the Chicago monetary School (headed by the well-known economist Milton Friedman) where a number of technocrats who occupied leading positions in the Chilean economy had studied and whose monetary theory was akin to the idea of shock therapy.

Upon being asked what I thought of these fears, and given my own observations, I replied that should the Chilean economy continue to demonstrate the good performance of recent years, his apprehensions were unfounded. I then ventured to ask my interlocutor which of the two fears worried him more. He answered with a laugh: "The fellows who made their studies at Chicago." It would seem, however, that reality has proved the contrary to be the case, which does happen with the opinions of other politicians as well. History has shown that Chile's experience has had excellent results.

- Setting up a legislative framework required for the functioning of a competitive free market economy;
- Price liberalization so that prices may be determined by the market forces;
- Rapid privatization of state property;
- Abolition of subsidies and establishing a strict budgetary discipline in order to achieve a significant deficit reduction;
- Denying bank credit to inefficient enterprises;
- Strict monetary control in order to prevent an excess in the money supply;
- Increasing use of the financial-banking instruments to promote the development of the private sector;
- Devaluation of the national currency in conformity with the real performance of the economy, and transition to convertibility;
- Working out of a social safety net program to stave off the negative consequences of the process of privatization;
- Securing of substantial foreign financing in order to bolster the national currency and the entire reform process.

The list, of course, is not exhaustive. It is only <u>indicative</u> of what type of measures are required.

The order in which these ideas are presented has also an indicative nature only. With regard to shock therapy we should distinguish a shock therapy program for economic stabilization with a limited number of objectives (this is not to be confused with a gradual therapy), in contrast to a global shock therapy which assumes its sudden implementation in all possible directions in order to build a market economy.

Not surprisingly, the limited "list" of objectives mentioned above was not warmly embraced by the population of these countries, but only as an emergency solution to put an end to a crisis of immeasurable consequences.

As will be seen later, the author's concern was not being confronted with a Hamletian dilemma "to use or not to use" shock therapy, but only whether the preexisting conditions for its successful implementation exist and how should it be applied to specific situations.

Shock therapy was accepted by the peoples of ex-communist countries who began building a free market economy for the following two reasons:

a) the austerity period required for its was considered to be 2-3 years at the most, while a gradual therapy implied a longer period of austerity, bringing with it the risk of hyper-inflation and massive unemployment, with serious political consequences;

b) the national leaders promoting shock therapy have not only legitimized their political position in general elections, but also enjoyed a total trust from the masses who supported them.

Without any doubt, the shock therapy was necessary in these countries for their future political life in order to destroy as quickly as possible the previous monolithic party structure and its bureaucratic apparatus, the so-called communist "nomenclature." It was also urgently necessary to build a legal framework for the transition period from the centralized planning system to a market economy.

However, the introduction of shock therapy in economic activity, which implies numerous socio-economic interconnections with multiple financial aspects is a very sensitive matter. It should be applied very carefully, otherwise it could hurt the promoters of these reforms and play into the hands of their adversaries, as proved to be the case in Russia, Poland, Hungary, etc.

## B. The Preliminary Results of Applying Shock Therapy in Some Ex-Communist Countries (A Critical Review)

Retrospective economic analysis of the past 2-3 years since shock therapy has been applied in these countries regrettably shows just such a negative trend. In most of these former communist countries, both industrial production and agricultural output have fallen drastically. Unemployment has rise rapidly. Broad worker unrest has taken place, and with some exception, inflation has continued at an unacceptable level.

Success as regards privatization is also questionable, with the exception of the former East Germany (for reason well known) and Hungary, where the reform was started much earlier. Moreover, despite price liberalization, all these countries, although endowed with important natural resources, especially in the field of agriculture, have experienced not only shortfalls in the supply of staples, but also the absence of a competitive environment (a possible exception was Hungary). Prices, prohibitive at times, ceased to be a signal from the market for a better allocation of resources, both physically and financially. These factors keep foreign investors, no doubt, at a distance.

True, in 1994, some progress was recorded in certain of these countries. In Poland, for instance, a growth of over four percent was recorded in the Gross National Product (GNP), but there were also serious political upheavals which call into question the 1994 results. In the Czech Republic the GNP has registered zero growth, which is surely cause for discouragement. Remarkable though is the fact that despite this economic stagnation, unemployment has remained stationary at 3.5% (as a result of some inefficient enterprises being kept afloat via subsidies), and a balanced budget was achieved.

Yet analysts are also asking themselves if these positive performance will be repeated. They ascribed the success of 1993, besides the advantages enjoyed by the Czech Republic (of which we will speak more later), to the excellent results in the field of tourism, which has brought in $1.3 billion. At the same time, there are also pessimistic apprehensions regarding unemployment.

In Hungary, for instance, whose results placed it for a while in the forefront of the reforming countries, the state of affairs has deteriorated since 1992 and the country has to face unexpected difficulties in its development. In this regard, the Table 1 speaks for itself. (See page 23.)

Therefore, these small positive results cannot cover the fact that the manner in which the shock therapy was applied offers, at least for the moment and after four years (1989-1993), an unpromising prospect. The fact cannot be ignored that due to this manner of application, Czechoslovakia was divided on January 1, 1993.

In Poland, in the elections of autumn 1993, Lech Walesa was forced to accept the defeat of the reformists and cooperate with a prime minister who was a member of the former Communist Party (renamed the Democratic Alliance of the Left). Presently Walesa is no longer president of Poland; the new president is a former communist.

**TABLE 1**

**COMPARATIVE TABLE OF FOUR
MACROECONOMIC INDICATORS (%)**

| | Industrial Production % | | | Inflation % | | |
|---|---|---|---|---|---|---|
| | 1992 | 1993 | 1993 | 1992 | 1993 | 1993 |
| | | Sem. I | Forecast | | Sem. I | Forecast |
| **Bulgaria** | -18.0 | -9.0 | -8 | 80.0 | 79.5 | 85.0 |
| **Czech Republic** | -10.6 | -4.6 | -2.0(c) | 11.1 | 21.7 | 20.0 |
| **Poland** | 4.2 | 9.4 | 4.0 | 43.0 | 38.0 | 37.0 |
| **Romania** | -22.1 | -7.5 | -6.0 | 210.4 | 194.4 | 205.0 |
| **Slovak Republic** | -12.9 | -10.0(d) | -8.0(d) | 10.0 | 21.6 | 30.0 |
| **Hungary** | -10.0 | 0.8(b) | -1.0 | 23.0 | 23.2 | 23.0 |

| | Real Wages (% growth) | | Retail Volume (% growth) | |
|---|---|---|---|---|
| | 1992 | 1993 | 1992 | 1993 |
| | | Sem. I | | Sem. I |
| **Bulgaria** | 15.0 | -11.1(a) | -32.2 | -15.2(b) |
| **Czech Republic** | 10.0 | 1.4(d) | 14.2 | 1.1(d) |
| **Poland** | -2.0 | 0.4 | -8.0 | 0.0(b) |
| **Romania** | -15.0 | -13.3 | -17.5 | -24.0 |
| **Slovak Republic** | 9.3 | 3.9(a) | 15.0 | 8.0(a) |
| **Hungary** | 2.4 | -0.2(b) | -2.5 | -3.5(b) |

Source: European Intelligence Unit, in "Business Central Europe" (1993), p. 14.

a) January-March
b) January-May
c) Last anticipation: zero growth
d) January-April

In Bulgaria, the Socialist Party (in reality the former Communist Party) in coalition with another small party, took control of the government. Yugoslavia practically has ceased to exist. In Russia, the reformists have been defeated, and it is not known what will happen with the reform; the situation could be described as "chaotic," to say the least.* On the whole, the outcome in Romania in 1994 was also unsatisfactory, and the political and economic developments remain uncertain.

Some politicians, economic advisors (local or from the West), the representatives of international financial agencies, and so on, might be surprised by these "negative" performances. Others could say that "it was to be expected, more or less, to turn out this way, but soon things will turn for the better." Many countries have, no doubt, gone through a number of difficult years, and the population may well accept such promises for a while. The tragedy consists in the fact that this slogan has been reiterated in the former communist countries year after year for almost half a century (and in Russia for nearly three quarters of a century). Two or three generations have known only sacrifice, famine, and oppression. It is very difficult to tell these people to bear it "just a little longer." The peoples in these countries do not want to wait any longer. After decades of relinquishment and deprivation, they have reached a threshold of social explosion.

This is a dangerous atmosphere. Not only may the very idea of reform be discredited, but it could cripple the entire effort aimed at making these reforms a success.

The economic and political outcomes mentioned above raise the following simple questions:

1. Was the shock therapy adequate? (keeping in mind the social and economic conditions prevailing in these countries at the time);
2. Are there certain preconditions necessary for a successful application of shock therapy, and what are these conditions?

---

* In the general elections of December 1993, the tidal wave of discontent expressed itself by placing an ultra-nationalist party led by Zhirinovsky ahead of everybody else. His program aims, one way or another, at the resurgence of Russian imperialism. In the elections of December 1995, the Communist Party placed first, followed by Zhirinovsky's party.

Let's try to answer these questions briefly. Shock therapy is necessary but it can only yield results when certain preconditions are met. Considering that political democracy has been achieved following the 1989 revolutions (although this assumption as regards some of these countries is not so much optimistic as it is rather naive), the following preconditions should have been present for shock therapy to be successful:

1. The existence of a private, more or less developed sector in agriculture (including the processing of certain agriculture products) as well as in the retail trade and some kind of services that would allow the carrying on of an incipient form of competitiveness, and a clear and unambiguous definition of private property, with all the practical and legal guarantees.
2. The availability of a technical, economic and especially of a massive financial assistance on the part of the industrially developed countries aiming to promote a program of economic stabilization in order to achieve price liberalization, privatization, professional requalification and possible relocation, as well as monetary convertibility.
3. The existence of an incipient form of a private banking system, which should slowly evolve into an organized banking system (not commercial banks which are in fact extensions of the central banks).
4. An entrepreneurial spirit in the true Western sense of the word (not of a petty peddler's mentality) that acknowledges both risk and profit as the most important driving factors in a free market economy.

These preconditions existed in the former West Germany, Chile and other countries. None of these preconditions were present in Eastern and Central Europe, with the exception of Poland and Hungary, where some of them were present. Although, as indicated in the preceding chapter, the legal framework to facilitate the transition has been set up rapidly enough, the experience has shown that this framework was not sufficient to compensate for the absence of the above-mentioned preconditions.*

Following the elections in Poland and Russia, it seems that the ranks of those voicing criticisms of the manner in which shock therapy has been implemented have increased, and new arguments were presented, such as:

a) Shock therapy exerts particularly strong financial pressures, considered by some as being similar to the pressures exerted on Germany after World War I, resulting in tragic political consequences;

b) "Transplanting" of shock therapy is taking place not only in the absence of a competitive market (in fact, it is a market under the control of state monopolies), but also in the absence of a mobile labor force; the private sector is deprived of adequate support, left to the mercy of the existing bureaucracy and affected by the lack of a domestic financial market. The expected financial help from the Western countries proves to be inadequate, both in volume terms and in the length of time needed to obtain it for a successful implementation of shock therapy;

c) The rise in prices, resulting from their "liberalization" and not the effect of market forces but of government measures, has led to rampant inflation combined with a scarcity of goods. A lot of goods became out of reach for the population, increasing its dissatisfaction and its opposition to reform;

d) Even if some prices were temporarily lowered, conditions existed for a new escalation (due to the overall economic, financial and political situation). These forces acted in a negative way on wage agreements, pushing a new wave of price increases.

e) A policy of greatly restricting credit especially hurts small enterprises, while the large state enterprises are able to avoid it through their well-preserved connections with the political moguls and via threats of massive layoffs.

---

* These were the main ideas I presented at the Conference of the National Association of Business Economists in September 1992 held in Dallas, Texas.

It is clear today that the operation euphemistically called "transplant" has been, one way or another, rejected by the economic organism due to the manner in which it was performed. Taking into account some previously analyzed objective and subjective factors may allow the avoidance of the rejection process, or to successfully confront it. As a matter of fact, specialized literature shows us that especially during the last two years, reservations were expressed (some by this author as early as 1990) as to the manner in which shock therapy should be implemented. This referred to a delimitation of its range of action and of a gradual approach regarding privatization of the big industrial enterprises, monetary convertibility, etc. Those who formulated these reservations emphasized that these could be accepted and even be necessary as long as <u>the reform process is kept at a brisk pace</u> and are not used as an excuse to justify procrastination regarding urgently needed changes.

Analyzing how strictly the shock therapy was applied in the former communist countries under discussion, we may have some surprises. In fact, only two countries have implemented shock therapy more or less strictly. We have in mind the former East Germany, able to apply the necessary measures thanks to the almost unlimited support of the former West Germany, which continues to pay even now the price of reunification (a price worth paying). The second is Poland, which disposed of an extensive private sector in agriculture and has received substantial foreign financial support.

The situation is somewhat different regarding other countries. In Hungary, where the experiment of transforming the "system" had begun as early as 1968, we may refer to a gradual approach, rather than a shock one. Over the years Hungary has transformed its monolithic monetary and banking system into a competitive, pluralistic one. It has gradually introduced more liberal trade and foreign investment regulations, a tax system favorable to economic development and has set up a framework for a financial market, first for government bond transactions and later for transactions in shares.

In the other countries, the Polish model was also corrected to have a more gradual approach. Before splitting up, the Czech Republic seemed to veer more decisively toward shock therapy, based on the existence of a number of favorable conditions.* But according

---

* E.g., a broad concentration of highly educated population, the geographic location, a small territory, its good reputation in the West.

to the *New York Times* of January 31, 1994, Vaclav Klaus was implementing a gradual program of reform instead of a shock therapy. Romania has somewhat modified the Polish model in its program of price liberalization and in its attempts to achieve convertibility, it has introduced a controlled "variable exchange rate." Bulgaria is also gradually implementing measures of trade liberalization.

In Russia, the main proponents of economic reform have long ago resigned from the government. Victor S. Chernomyrdin, the prime minister, had declared himself in favor of gradual reform as far back as 1993. It is difficult to quantify at this time the negative impact of the election results of 1995. But it is obvious that the Russian proponents of economic reform have asked the citizenry for too many sacrifices, some of which could have probably been avoided.

As it was stressed earlier, most of the positive and negative evaluations of shock therapy refer to the methods of its implementation, and do not question its very necessity. Practical experience shows that certain preconditions are needed in order to apply shock therapy, as well as an urgency for some measures to amend it, which could differ from one country to another during the process of implementation.[†]

At the present time, more or less, the necessary preconditions for shock therapy are present in all the former communist countries of Central and Eastern Europe. It is certainly to be regretted that it has taken so long for these preconditions to be created, with so many material and moral sacrifices, which have not yet come to an end. And here lies the most serious danger. Now, when the overall circumstances would allow the transition to be resolutely tackled, the necessary measures could be met by the population without the enthusiasm that had greeted the 1989 revolution. They could be met with the indifference and apathy that all too often follow unfulfilled expectations or, even worse, with a stubborn opposition to any kind of reform.

---

[†] In this context and in order not to extend this chapter unduly, I shall give in Addendum 1 the text of an article I had submitted to the *New York Times* on March 1, 1992, under the title "Economic shock therapy program should be amended." Regrettably, the paper did not publish it. It was probably my mistake to have sent it too soon; I should have sent it in 1994. Indeed, at the end of 1993, the *New York Times* printed on its front page an article with a sensational title that the United States has given up on the shock therapy for Russia.

Because of this, the present period in Romania's development towards a market economy is possibly the most <u>critical</u>, and the acceptance of one program over another for the pursuit of reform assumes a special importance. In this respect, please let us further discuss my proposal concerning a mixed therapy.

## C. THE NECESSITY FOR A MIXED THERAPY

Toward the end of 1990, the author, as President of the Romanian-American Chamber of Commerce of New York, organized in Bucharest a seminar on the problems of privatization. The main topic of his paper was a proposal for a "mixed therapy," an idea which now seems to be applicable not only in Romania but in other countries as well.

In the paper it was emphasized that in the application of shock therapy certain gradualistic actions are necessary and therefore a special care is required on the part of reformers so as not to trigger undesirable social and political processes by their economic measures. It follows that the manner in which this gradualistic process is understood acquires particular importance. This should not be seen as a bureaucratic policy of procrastination in creating a market economy. If so, we speak in different idioms.

In our understanding, gradual therapy refers to the step by step implementation of a steadfast policy aimed at a maxi-privatization (on which we will speak later), <u>whence</u> it ought to begin, and <u>how</u> it should be applied as swiftly as possible, so as to avoid the risk of hyper-inflation. In this meaning, it becomes an intrinsic part of the author's "mixed therapy" proposal.

The experience in Poland, where shock therapy was applied, and the one in Hungary where gradual therapy was used, show that neither of these solutions should be viewed as absolute; neither ought to be rejected either, but they should be combined within the framework of a "mixed therapy."

As regards the concept of "mixed therapy," it should be defined more precisely because it may suggest in the mind of the adversaries of reform that it is a pleading in favor of maintaining the "state property," well known to be bankrupt to a great extent. In our understanding, "mixed therapy" has nothing in common with such thinking. On the contrary, it aims mainly at the gradual (and the sooner the better) decrease of the presence of the state in the country's economy under whatever guise, as owner, administrator, contractor, etc.

If not properly explained, this concept could also be understood as a rather questionable term by certain international financial institutions such as the International Monetary Fund or the World Bank, and for this reason, the former communist countries, who are facing enough difficulties when applying for financial resources, do not wish to engage in linguistic disputes with the IMF and others. Yet it appears that even these institutions have begun to show some flexibility in observing of the so-called "conditionality" – or to put it more simply, in the problems of "gradualism" (in the meaning presented above) – especially following the political events in Russia. Therefore, this apprehension is no longer justified, once gradualism is perceived as an adversary of procrastination or of unjustified postponements, and when its implementation does not negatively affect the speed of the reform process, including monetary and budgetary restraint. Also very important is that a mixed therapy can much better cope with the complex problems raised by the need for social protection.

In our view, mixed therapy is a combination of two models: a model of <u>mini-privatization</u> and another of <u>maxi-privatization</u>. The first model must concentrate on agriculture, on the production of consumer goods, on the retail trade, and on the services sector, all subject to a program of shock therapy having two principal goals:

1. To stimulate the migration of the labor force from the giant, inefficient state enterprises to the privatized small and medium-sized units, as well as from cities to villages. In this way the private sector will be strengthened and unemployment reduced;
2. To control excess liquidity within the system while avoiding painful blows to the population, as happened in the past, such as: the arbitrary price hike, confiscation of cash through tricky "monetary reform," or the wasteful use of hard currency in unproductive transactions. These liquidities, attracted <u>voluntarily</u> from the population, could be used in promoting mini-privatization through internal means and reduce inflation expectations.

The second model concerning maxi-privatization implies a gradual, but as rapidly as possible, reorganization and/or restructuring of the big state enterprises, setting up a special budget for their privatization, and laying ground for a functional capital market aimed at attracting foreign investors in this process. It is clear that maxi-privatization, however rapid, is a longer process. Without an extensive attraction of foreign capital, a real maxi-privatization (and not one achieved by giving out certificates or vouchers) is impossible to achieve in these countries.

Industrialized countries in the West will support such a program on the condition that it is prepared with great care and responsibility.

If it is possible to make historical comparisons, regardless of an economic and political environment totally different, we can say that the ex-communist countries find themselves now at a crossroad that the Western countries faced in the 1930s. At that time, the struggle between the advocates of "laissez-faire" and those of the command, totalitarian economy was won by the advocates of the middle course, such as Keynes and his followers. They made use of financial and monetary means and fiscal policy in order to preserve the free market and human freedoms. In the case of the former communist countries, once the totalitarian political and economic structures have been destroyed, this middle course could be a solution of the type of "mixed therapy" which I have attempted to describe.

Due to the insufficient statistical data required for this type of analysis, we do not pretend to be in a position to finalize adequately this theory, but only to present it in its proper framework within the overall process of transition.

# III

---

# THE ECONOMIC REFORM IN ROMANIA FOR A FREE MARKET ECONOMY

## A. GENERAL CONSIDERATIONS

It seems to be unanimously accepted that the reform during the transition period consists of two programs whose sequence, interference or overlapping – for a variety reasons, tactical or strategic – could not be ignored, both for the theoretical analysis and the practical activity. These programs are known as:

- The stabilization program of the reform which essentially implies, more or less, the implementation of shock therapy which, at the end of the previous chapter, I have included within the framework of "mixed therapy" as the mini-privatization model;
- The structural reforms program which I have included in the framework of "mixed therapy" as a maxi-privatization model.

It should be emphasized again that this separation is for the purpose of theoretical analysis only. In fact, economic reality imposes this separation to be in a state of continuous interconditioning.

The implementation of these programs, whatever their name, implies a clear definition of private property and of privatization, valid for both internal and external economic agents. It also implies the reinventing of the price mechanism, as well as of the budgetary, financial, banking, and monetary systems, getting rid of bureaucratic obstructions, and devising a strong social safety net. Going further, it is necessary to set up a kind of "general scheme" that would make clear the directions and possible ramifications for advancing towards a market economy.

At the seminar on the subject of privatization held in Bucharest, the author made a proposal regarding a "General Scheme," its phases (and within these, their respective stages), as well as the sequences (i.e., the priorities in each phase or stage respectively), and of concrete measures which should be applied in this respect. This proposal should have found its place here, because after almost four years, it has not become out of date. However, a number of suggestions made in 1990 have already been put into effect. It would be more useful to give the text unchanged in Addendum 2 and refer to it when necessary.

Instead, here is the place for adding a number of newly emerged aspects and also to enlarge upon a series of problems which, for lack of time, were not discussed at that seminar. Briefly, the phases described in Addendum 2 are the following:

1. The documentary evidence-gathering phase which would allow us to obtain as complete as possible an image, in quantitative and value form, of the material (under whatever guise), financial, and human resources. In accordance with their number, their structure by various economic, financial, social, and national security criteria, we may be in a position to define strategic decisions concerning both the privatization process (where, when, how, and, if need be, with whom) and that of restructuring the economy from the point of view of profitability and efficiency.

2. The phase of positioning the mechanisms required for the functioning of a free market economy. This phase has two stages:
   - The first stage aims at bringing into operation the necessary legislation for this type of economy as well as certain financial, banking, monetary, budgetary and currency instruments indispensable for a market economy, opening the stage of the privatization process and building up a social safety net.
   - A second stage goes further and aims at accelerating the process of privatization, giving assistance to private banks, setting up the framework for the appearance of a capital market and of the institutions connected with it. Also, it aims at the liberalization, broadly speaking, of the price system already initiated in the first stage, abolition of budget subsidies, introduction of a credit policy that would not only strengthen the private sector, but also encourage competition within its framework and its relations with the state sector, and intensify the efforts to attract foreign capital. The second stage would also

introduce a system of bookkeeping in line with international standards and with the system of statistical
reports both at the macro- and microeconomic levels.
3. The take-off phase, so-called because in this phase, if the
economic market mechanisms have been properly laid
out, the necessary conditions exist for the economy to
jump thanks to the absence of direct state intervention in
the management of enterprises, the reintegration of
Romania within the world economic and financial
markets, its access to international commercial banks,
the creation of a necessary framework for achieving
monetary convertibility, and so on.

Of course, the second phase, with its two stages, where the
most diverse and divergent interests will have to be reconciled
democratically, is at the core of the entire operation and will be the
most difficult to go through.

In Addendum 2 estimates are given as to the duration of each
phase and stage respectively. They were suggested in 1990, when it
was considered – in case they would have been initiated at once – that
their implementation would require less than four years. As is well
known, things have taken a different course, and our proposal made
at that time did not find an audience in Romania.*

Before approaching critically certain aspects of the sequence in
which the transition process unfolded, it would be useful to present
briefly the context in which the reform process was begun in Romania, as this explains some of the author's positions and proposals.

## B. SOME CRITICAL VIEWS ON THE BEGINNING OF THE REFORM

In comparison with its neighbors, Romania entered the path of
reform in particularly favorable circumstances. From a political
point of view, it was the only former communist country in the area
that "punished" by execution the dictatorial couple. It also started
1990 without foreign debts, with a surplus in its balance of trade and

---

* I should like to mention that the "General Scheme" had been very well received
by Professor Jacques Attali, at the time Chairman of the European Bank for Reconstruction and Development (EBRD), with headquarters in London.

current accounts, and with a remarkably large quantity of foreign currency reserves. At that time the Romanian monetary unit (the Leu) was quoted very favorably on the secondary financial market in the West. How it was possible to pass in only a few years to negative data for all the indicators mentioned above, without a marked improvement internally, is a question that deserves a serious and responsible analysis, but it is not the purpose of this work.

There are many explanations, both objective and especially subjective. In the author's opinion the main explanation rests in the way in which shock therapy was implemented. This means its priorities, the concept that stood at the foundation of privatization, the role of the human element, the prevailing negative mentality on profit, and the overall political background of insecurity.

Could it have been done differently? In an interview given by the author in May 1993 for the newspaper *Meridian* (Bucharest), the answer was: YES. A better, more efficient alternative for the transition process could have been chosen. In connection with this choice, it is often put forward that a selection of the optimum variant did not rest only with Romania and that "in fact" it was the International Monetary Fund or the World Bank which had the final say in the matter. Without denying the part played by these international financial institutions in the decision-making process that faced Romania, the country's favorable position at the beginning of 1990 (compared with that of its neighbors) for negotiations with the above-mentioned institutions cannot be ignored. Another favorable fact was that Romania was, at that time, the only country among the ex-communist states that was a member of the International Monetary Fund and had a very good foreign debt payment record (for which the Romanian people had paid a heavy price). Therefore, Romania had, relatively speaking, a strong position for obtaining much more favorable conditions in these negotiations.*

The following table (pp. 36-39) provides a comparative view of the macroeconomic situation of Romania and her neighboring countries. (The table is a summary of one published by the *Financial Times* on January 24, 1990). Some indicators were not included

---

* In a special article entitled "Eastern Europe in Ferment" (January 24, 1990), the *Financial Times*, referring to conditions in Romania, wrote: "Ironically, had it wished to, Romania could have had immediate access to multilateral, bilateral or trade financing now that the interdiction to contract new foreign loans had been lifted."

either because they were derived from those already presented in the table, or because their economic relevance was debatable. (For instance, those regarding the increase in consumer prices and real wages. It is well known that these indicators were distorted in order to hide inflation and the real standard of living.)

The analysis that follows on the liberalization of prices and the privatization process shows that, in Romania, the sequence in which the shock therapy had been applied did not match the real local conditions. Had there been enough determination, it should have been possible to introduce some corrections in the course of economic reform. An appropriate time for such a reexamination within the general framework of the reform would have been with the investiture of a new government in 1991. Unfortunately, the prime minister stated publicly that his only purpose was to continue the existing program, when in fact the problem was to <u>correct</u> it. (Actually, the brief period of the Stolojan government up to the 1992 elections would not have made possible such an action, but the very debate would have been positive in the given situation.)

The main objection regarding the sequence of reform in Romania concerns price liberalization. The topic has been discussed by the author in a special paper presented at a seminar in Bucharest in 1990 expressing his criticism in general terms only (see Addendum 2). He returned to this subject again in an interview given to the daily newspaper *Libertatea* on March 29, 1991.

As is known, at the end of 1990 and during 1991, despite critical shortages of the most elementary goods and skyrocketing inflation, shock therapy in Romania (and other ex-communist countries) started with price "liberalization." The new "free" prices were not set by competition – which did not exist as yet – but by the state, as in the past. The presumption behind this dangerous move was that prices, after going through the roof for a short time, would head back down due to increasing competitive supply and declining demand. Though theoretically correct for a competitive market, this presumption proved totally <u>unrealistic</u> in a country which had long been under dictatorship and where a competitive environment could not be created overnight.

**TABLE 2**
**A COMPARATIVE TABLE OF IMPORTANT**
**STATISTICAL INDICATORS AT THE END OF 1988**

| | Bulgaria | Czecho-slovakia | East Germany | Poland | Romania | Hungary |
|---|---|---|---|---|---|---|
| **General Statistics** | | | | | | |
| Surface (sq. km.) | 110.912 | 127.905 | 108.333 | 304.463 | 237.500 | 93.033 |
| Population (mill.) | 9.0 | 15.5 | 16.6 | 37.9 | 23.1 | 10.7 |
| GDP ($ bn.) | 38 | 18 | 209 | 69 | 71 | 28 |
| GDP per capita ($ thous.) | 4244 | 7591 | 12608 | 1818 | 3072 | 2621 |
| **Balance of Payments in Convertible Currency** | | | | | | |
| Trade Balance ($ bn.) | -1.3 | -0.1 | 0.1 | 1.0 | 3.8 | 0.7 |
| Current Account | -1.5 | -0.3 | 0.6 | -0.6 | 3.5 | -0.6 |
| Exports in convertible currency ($ bn.) | 3.2 | 5.8 | 10.4 | 7.7 | 7.7 | 5.9 |
| Imports in convertible currency ($ bn.) | 4.5 | 5.9 | 10.3 | 6.7 | 3.9 | 5.2 |
| Total exports ($ bn.) | 17.22 | 24.94 | 32.05 | 13.96 | 12.90 | 10.00 |
| Total imports ($ bn.) | 16.58 | 24.26 | 31.12 | 12.16 | 9.50 | 9.37 |
| **Exports and Imports Volume (Annual % change 1988/87)** | | | | | | |
| | Bulgaria | Czecho-slovakia | East Germany | Poland | Romania | Hungary |
| Exports | 3.6 | -4.0 | 1.0 | 9.4 | 9.3 | 5.2 |
| Imports | 0.7 | 3.0 | 3.3 | 8.7 | 4.4 | -1.9 |

| Exports and Imports Value (Annual % change 1988/87) | | | | | |
| --- | --- | --- | --- | --- | --- |
| | Bulgaria | Czecho-slovakia | East Germany | Poland | Romania | Hungary |
| Exports | 8.6 | 8.5 | 2.6 | 14.3 | 11.8 | 4.4 |
| Imports | 2.6 | 4.4 | 2.7 | 12.1 | 3.0 | -5.0 |

| Regional Trade Structure (1988 % share) | | | | | | |
| --- | --- | --- | --- | --- | --- | --- |
| **Eastern Europe** | | | | | | |
| Exports | 18.1 | 29.9 | 26.5 | 16.2 | 16.4 | 17.0 |
| Imports | 20.1 | 32.3 | 24.8 | 17.2 | 21.3 | 18.7 |
| **Soviet Union** | | | | | | |
| Exports | 62.8 | 43.1 | 35.5 | 24.5 | 23.4 | 27.6 |
| Imports | 53.7 | 40.4 | 34.6 | 23.4 | 30.9 | 25.0 |
| **Developed Countries** | | | | | | |
| Exports | 6.4 | 16.3 | 29.9 | 43.3 | 37.9 | 40.5 |
| Imports | 15.5 | 18.6 | 33.2 | 45.7 | 11.6 | 43.6 |
| **Developing Countries and Others** | | | | | | |
| Exports | 12.8 | 10.8 | 8.1 | 16.0 | 22.3 | 14.9 |
| Imports | 10.6 | 8.8 | 7.4 | 13.7 | 36.2 | 12.7 |

| Debt | | | | | | |
| --- | --- | --- | --- | --- | --- | --- |
| Gross debt ($bn.) | 7.6 | 5.1 | 19.9 | 3.9 | 2.7 | 17.3 |
| % of GDP | 20.0 | 4.3 | 9.5 | 56.4 | 3.8 | 61.8 |
| Net debt ($ bn.) | 6.6 | 3.4 | 10.2 | 35.3 | 1.3 | 16.1 |

| Debt Index (1980=100) | | | | | | |
| --- | --- | --- | --- | --- | --- | --- |
| Gross debt 1988 | 211 | 113 | 146 | 161 | 28 | 190 |
| Net debt 1988 | 227 | 103 | 87.9 | 150.2 | 14.0 | 209.1 |

| Growth of industrial and agriculture production (% change 1988/87) | | | | | | |
| --- | --- | --- | --- | --- | --- | --- |
| Gross industrial product | 5.2 | 2.0 | 3.7 | 5.4 | 3.6 | 3.5 (1987) |
| Gross agricultural output | -0.1 | 2.2 | -4.0 | 0.6 | 2.9 | 4.5 |

Source: The Economic Commission for Europe (ECE), Secretariat Common Data Base, compiled from national reports of the COMECON statistics. Published by the *Financial Times*, January 24, 1990, p. 9.

Therefore, it is very important to analyze the interrelation between the privatization and liberalization of the price system. Can a price liberalization be sustained without massive privatization and vice versa? According to the painful experience in some of these countries, this question is really a fundamental one. In our opinion, one cannot give one more importance than the other because they are essentially two sides of the same coin, i.e., a market economy. It does not make sense to liberalize prices without an extensive private sector and strong competition among its units and, given this environment, it does not make sense to keep price determination centralized. From this thesis, we could draw some conclusions for the former communist countries where the problem of privatization is of paramount importance.

First, we have to underline the fact that in most of these countries, almost everything was nationalized until 1990. In their move to a market economy, they have to carefully maintain a sensitive equilibrium between privatization and price liberalization in every sector. Price liberalization by the state in the consumer goods sector without a large private sector to produce and sell them competitively will inevitably result in artificial prices – completely unrelated to supply and demand – which would then require some central intervention to keep inflation from getting out of hand. At the same time, if privatization occurs in some sectors of the economy beyond the absorptive capacity of the consuming sector (both internal and external) massive unemployment, which may be very difficult to correct later on, could result. Of course, in all of these countries, given the prior economic structure, it will be impossible to completely avoid higher inflation and unemployment, but measures can be taken to make this process less painful.

Second, due to the required equilibrium pointed out earlier, should shock therapy be deemed necessary, such a therapy should be applied simultaneously in both areas: privatization and price liberalization. A delay in one side or the other will very soon undermine the goals for which this therapy was applied in the first place. Unfortunately, in the ex-communist countries mentioned above, this requirement was generally disregarded and consequently hyper-inflation and massive currency depreciation ensued.

Third, due to the existing conditions in these countries with a huge and inefficient state sector for producing means of production and a relatively modest state sector producing consumer goods, it is not advisable to apply shock therapy on an economy-wide basis because big state enterprises cannot be privatized overnight. On the other hand, small and medium-sized enterprises producing consumer goods could be privatized much faster and could create a competitive environment for this segment of the economy.

This reality was more or less ignored in some of these countries, by some kind of proposals to speed up the privatization of big state enterprises through a kind of redistribution – free of charge – of a portion of their assets to an important part of the population. (In a separate chapter on privatization, the author will explain his misgivings about this decision.) Here the author would like only to stress the fact that the free distribution of a portion of assets (in the form of certificates of ownership or vouchers) does not increase the country's national wealth. Instead, it could become a potential cause for an unacceptable growth in the money supply with important inflationary consequences if there are shortfalls in the supply of necessary merchandise and/or a strong financial market to absorb these vouchers does not exist.

Ignoring the needed equilibrium between privatization and price liberalization could lead to an increase in the existing imbalances in the economy and reduce, in real terms, the expenses for social protection, due to inflation. Such a state of affairs also favors the growth of the euphemistically called "parallel" economy – previously known as the "black market" – which totally escapes financial control. The resulting tax evasion harms both the budgetary revenues by increasing the existing deficit and the population, which must pay higher taxes. We do not know what is the weight of the "parallel economy" in Romania, but it must be quite significant, judging by the fact that even in countries which are at a much higher level of economic development, such as Italy, for instance, it is estimated to account for at least 20% of the GNP.

Some might argue that the existence of a significant "parallel economy" indirectly reflects the growth of the private sector, and is thus a positive phenomenon. However, such a view would be gravely mistaken. This trend would be very dangerous, especially during the transition period. The black market has no relation to privatization. (As is well known, it was also quite significant in ex-communist economies due to the shortage of consumer goods.)

When we refer to the need for extending the private sector we have in mind a productive economic development which would favor

GNP growth, instead of eroding it, reduce unemployment in the state sector and push upwards the standard of living.

Last but not least in importance is the impact of price liberalization on the relation between prices and wages. In Romania the private sector is still too weak to generate a real labor market. On the other hand, the trade unions are getting stronger but they are yet unable to play as an important a role as they should in a market economy. As a result, wages are more often dictated "from above" than the result of negotiation (although the trade unions had some of their grievances met). Still, it is a fact that at present, wages cannot keep up with the movement of liberalized prices.

The following chart, which was first published in an article by I. Marcovici appearing in *Romania Libera* on January 13, 1994, is quite enlightening:

**The Lag between Consumer Prices and the Medium Income of Wage-Earners**

**October 1990 = 100**

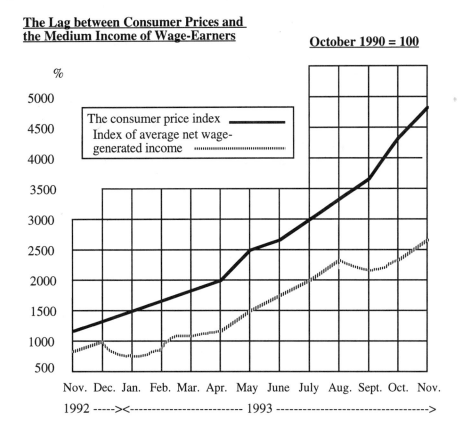

The increasing scissors between prices and wages could indirectly help to cover budgetary subsidies (to what extent we do not know) for inefficient state enterprises and therefore to diminish the budget deficit. At the same time, it has a negative impact on the main macroeconomic correlations and on the population's standard of living.

Before continuing our analysis, it would be useful to have a comparative picture of the development of reform in Romania and in other former communist countries of the same region. To this end, we have included an abbreviated version of a very interesting table published by the European Bank for Reconstruction and Development (EBRD) in its "Annual Economic Outlook" of September 1993. The EBRD table provided data for 25 countries, starting with Albania and ending with Uzbekistan. For our analysis we selected only the information about six former communist countries of Central and Eastern Europe: Bulgaria, the Czech Republic, Poland, Romania, the Slovak Republic, and Hungary (see **Table 3**, following pages). As can be seen from this table, there are many similarities and only minor differences in the development of reform in these six countries.

Caution is recommended for using these data because of possible differences in the perception of certain concepts used by one country or another, between methods of reporting, the computation of some statistical indicators, etc.

TABLE 3
A COMPARATIVE VIEW REGARDING THE REFORMS
IN SIX EX-COMMUNIST COUNTRIES

| | Bulgaria | Czech Republic | Hungary |
|---|---|---|---|
| **Reform Programs Initiated** | 1987 | January 1991 | 1968 - The New Economic Mechanism |
| **Property Restitution** | Urban property restitution largely completed; rural land restitution proceeding according to plan, about half of claims have been processed. | Mostly completed. | Yes, in progress. |
| **Small Privatization** | Just begun, but encountering problems with restitution. | Completed; 26,000 units sold. | Completed for 70% of small firms identified for privatization. |
| **Large Privatization** | 83 companies being prepared for privatization in 1993. | First wave completed: 2,300 firms (book value CSK 700 bn. = 100% of annual GDP). Multiple methods used including voucher privatization. | Large firms accounting for 18% of the book value of this group have been privatized. |
| **Bankruptcy Law** | Under preparation since 1991, but not expected to be passed by parliament until end 1993. | Partial implementation October 1991. Revised law implemented April 1993. | Law initiated January 1992. As of Dec. 1992, 2294 bankruptcy cases had begun judiciary proceedings. |
| **Banking Reform** | Two-tier banking system created over 1987-1991 period. Central Bank Act passed June 1991. Banking law passed March 1992. | Two-tier banking system January 1990. New banking laws February 1992. Series of measures to deal with bad debt. | Two-tier system established January 1987. Government began a programme to pay 50-70% of the face value of non-performing loans in the form of long-term bonds in Sept. 1992. Interest rate free. Significant presence of foreign banks. |
| **Comprehensive Programme Adopted** | February 1991 | January 1991 (while still part of Czechoslovakia) | 1988 |
| **New Commercial Law** | Laws dealing with accounting, competition, foreign investment, privatization, cooperatives and companies passed in 1992. | New code adopted January 1992. | New enterprise law enacted in 1992. |

| | Poland | Romania | Slovak Republic |
|---|---|---|---|
| **Reform Programs Initiated** | 1989 | 1990 | January 1991 |
| **Property Restitution** | Legislation for reprivatization of property seized by State 1944-89 in preparation; compensation or restitution is envisaged. | Yes. Difficulties and delays especially for land restitution. Still to resolve the problem of privately owned houses. | Mostly completed. |
| **Small Privatization** | Rate of small privatization high. Most assets of the few SOEs liquidated in 1992 were leased. | 2,300 SMEs to be privatized in 1993; accounts for 90% of retail outlets and 45% of retail trade. | Completed; 9,000 units sold. |
| **Large Privatization** | 600 firms identified for privatization as of summer 1993. Plan calls for 200 large firms to be transferred to 5-8 investment funds. Shares to be distributed to pensioners and public sector employees; 400 firms to be privatized more slowly through 15 additional funds, shares to be sold to general public. | 70% of farm land privatized. 15.5 million Certificates of Ownership (CO) distributed as of Dec. 1992. Estimated value for a CO is Lei 150,000. Plan calls for establishment of 5 funds to assume ownership of 6,200 identified firms. | First wave completed. 711 firms (book value CSK 168 bn. = 40% annual GDP) via voucher privatization. Multiple methods used including voucher privatization. |
| **Bankruptcy Law** | For private firms, old commercial code of 1934 reinforced. For SOEs, 1990 Law of State Enterprises governs bankruptcies. | Draft of the Bankruptcy Law submitted to Parliament. 1934 Commercial Code still in place. | Partial implementation Oct. 1991. Revised law implemented June 1993. |
| **Banking Reform** | Two-tier banking system in 1989. New Bank Act, 1992, gives Central Bank supervisory power and establishes prudential limits for commercial banks. New banking law under consideration. | Two-tier banking system since Sept. 1990. New Banking Laws 29 March 1991. | Two-tier banking system Jan. 1990. New banking laws Feb. 1992. Series of measure to deal with bad debt. |
| **Comprehensive Programme Adopted** | 1989 Balcerowicz Plan | April 1991 | January 1991 (while still part of Czechoslovakia) |
| **New Commercial Law** | Commercial code of 1934 applies to private firms. | 7 August 1990 law governs reorganizing commercial companies and 16 Nov. 1990 law details commercial code. | New code implemented Jan. 1992. |

| | Bulgaria | Czech Republic | Hungary |
|---|---|---|---|
| **Personal/Labor Tax Rates** Employer payroll | 42% | 45% | 51% |
| Income (top marginal rate): | 52% | 47% | 40% |
| Income (lowest positive rate) | 20% | 15% | 25% |
| VAT (standard) | 20% | 23% | 25% |
| **Corporate/ Investment Tax Rates** Corporate (Standard) | 40% | 45% | 40% |
| Capital gain tax rate (same as highest personal income tax rate) | 52% | 47% | 40% |
| **Foreign Trade Liberalization** | Most restrictions removed Feb. 1991. Exports restrictions and quotas still enforced on six primary commodities. Major overhaul of tariffs completed July 1992. | Import liberalization Jan. 1991. Average tariff rate 5%. Few quantitative restrictions on agriculture imports only. Few quantitative restrictions on exports. | Nominal average tariff (10.9%). Few quantitative restrictions on exports or imports. |
| **Treatment of Foreign Direct Investment** | Highly receptive to FDI but external debt stalemate and lack of confidence in economy serious constraints. Tax incentive part of package. | National treatment, no special incentives. | National treatment in 1991, incentives for foreign investors to be phased out by end of 1993. |
| **Exchange Rate Regime** | Lev freely floating since Feb. 1991. | Pegged to currency basket. Special clearing arrangement with Slovak Republic. Czech Crown introduced Feb. 1993 after monetary split. | Forint pegged to a basket in which the USD and DM have the same weight. |
| **Capital Account Convertibility** | Capital controls in place. | Capital controls in place. | Residents and non-residents can open foreign currency accounts. Enterprises (except joint ventures) may not hold foreign currency. Banks need special license to hold foreign currency. |

| | Poland | Romania | Slovak Republic |
|---|---|---|---|
| **Personal/Labor Tax Rates**<br><br>Employer payroll | 46% | 41% | 38% |
| Income (top marginal rate): | 40% | 45% | 47% |
| Income (lowest positive rate) | 20% | 6% | 19% |
| VAT (standard) | 22% | 18% | 26% |
| **Corporate/ Investment Tax Rates**<br><br>Corporate (Standard) | 40% | 30-60% | 45% |
| Capital gain tax rate (same as highest personal income tax rate) | 40% | 45% | 47% |
| **Foreign Trade Liberalization** | Average tariff rate 18.4%. Concessionary reciprocal trade arrangement made with the Visegrad group. No quantitative restrictions on either exports or imports. | Import/export liberalization in Jan. 1990. Import tariff rates between 10-30%, depending upon the product and the stage of processing. Some imports quantitative restriction. | Import liberalization Jan. 1991. Average tariff rate 5%. Few quantitative restrictions remain except on agricultural imports. Few quantitative restrictions on exports. |
| **Treatment of Foreign Direct Investment** | Until Dec. 1993 any foreign investor may apply for a tax exemption if the investment exceeds ECU 2 million. | Special incentives extended under 3/4 1991 law. Tax holidays for 2-5 years. Proposals submitted to Parliament to allow land ownership by foreigners under debate. | 1/4/1993 law extends a 1-year holiday to firms more than 30% foreign owned and further 2 years of reduced profit tax. New law differs from Czech national treatment policy. |
| **Exchange Rate Regime** | Crawling peg regime instituted in May 1991 with the rate of crawl 1.8% per month vis-a-vis the USD. | Managed float regime. | Pegged to currency basket. Special clearing arrangement with Czech Republic. Slovak Crown introduced Feb. 1993 after monetary split. |
| **Capital Account Convertibility** | Capital controls in place. | Capital controls in place. | Capital controls in place. |

## C. THE NEED FOR TRANSPARENCY IN THE DEFINITION OF PRIVATE PROPERTY

A market economy cannot exist without a private sector which would not only be capable of spontaneous and continuous growth but also of becoming a strong competitor to the public sector. This is why the correct definition of private property is of paramount importance.

In every country such a definition is usually provided by the basic law of the land, the Constitution. However, in the Western countries with a long tradition of property there are probably few people who look to the Constitution for this definition. The idea has been ingrained in the public consciousness such a long time that its essence is well understood. People in these countries are probably more concerned with their Civil Code which spells out in detail the content, framework, rights and obligations resulting from the right to property.

The situation is different in the former communist countries of Europe where private property has been relinquished for decades – people desperately tried to rid themselves of it so they would not be labeled "bourgeois" or "petit-bourgeois," and thus be branded as outcasts for life by the communist regime. Not surprisingly in these countries, there were endless debates regarding the concept of private property and the way it should be defined by the Constitution.

The Romanian Constitution does not provide a clear, transparent definition of this concept. When it refers to private property, the Constitution passed in 1992 uses several wordings which can lead to confusion. Chapter II, section 41, paragraph 1 mentions that the right to property as well as the restitution of the debts incurred by the state are guaranteed and that the content and limits of those rights are specified by law. Up to this point this definition could have been quite satisfactory but the next paragraph of the same article (paragraph 2) seems to differentiate between the general concept of property and a specific private property when it says: "private property enjoys equal protection under the law, irrespective of its owner." The word guaranteed is no longer present (my emphasis - D.G.).

Chapter VI, Title IV, section 135 stresses again the idea expressed in section 41, paragraph 2, which says that "the state protects property." Thus, the text of the Constitution which repeats twice the wording "protects property" (once specifically referring to private property) unavoidably leads to ambiguity with the term "guaranteed" used at first (with general applicability), because there are nuances in language between "to guarantee" and "to protect" private property. It is only the guaranteeing of this property that can insure the private owner that he really is an independent economic agent.

The consequences of this lack of precision will be seen in the next chapters and especially in the section regarding the Certificates of Ownership and later on in the analysis of the Law on the Land Fund. It is hard to comprehend why an economic system moving toward a market economy would maintain such an ambiguous definition, though this matter has been discussed many times in Parliament.

The need for economic independence is not a new discovery. It had been pointed out, more or less timidly, during the Communist dictatorship under the more limited label of "administrative autonomy." However this subtle linguistic distinction was not helpful.

In 1958-59, in a more "favorable" climate in Romania after the resumption of political relations with Yugoslavia,* the author, together with two other contributors, tried, in a veiled form, to criticize the idea of centralized state management in a book that they intended to publish. The title of the book was *The Economic Management of Industrial Enterprises*. The first show of independence was that the authors renounced the hated word "khozrashchiot," taken from the Russian language, which no one understood in Romania. But this first show of independence was also the last one. The book touched upon two ideas which were considered heresies at that time. The first was about the need to insure real autonomy for the enterprise managers, which was interpreted as being critical of centralized (supposedly democratic) management. The second idea was that profit is the real indicator of economic efficiency, which went even more against the foundations of Marxism. Thought the book was printed and ready for distribution to the bookstores by the Scientific Publishing House in Bucharest, not only was it ordered

---

* At that time Yugoslavia was promoting a kind of anti-Stalinist socialist "model" which in the last resort proved to just as bankrupt.

taken off the list of future publications, but the proof itself was ordered to be melted.

At present, when according to official statements in Romania that the pillars of totalitarianism have been crushed, there is supposed to be a real autonomy as well as a real independence for owners, managers, etc. This independence conferred by the right of ownership must be unconditionally guaranteed. How can this be achieved? Research in this field offers the following suggestions:[*]

a) The introduction of a constitutional amendment when there are ambiguities regarding the guarantee of private ownership in the existing Constitution;

b) Clearly specifying the circumstances under which the right to ownership can be restricted – the legal provisions when such restriction is warranted, for instance of serious national security considerations or when there are very well-established public interest reasons, etc. (The more imprecise the specification of the circumstances when this right can be restricted, the more numerous the venues for its infringement and the greater the investor's risk);

c) Appropriate legislation to provide the private owner with full power of decision regarding the way he manages his company, the freedom to start or close down a business, to start or end his activity at will, to act according to his own interests. The government must specify in precise terms when some of its regulations can affect the above-mentioned rights and under what specific circumstances;

d) In order to strengthen the private sector, the government must assure the entrepreneurs that it will not make use of its financial and economic levers to protect the public sector or to create an unfavorable environment for private enterprises in terms of competitiveness, which

---

[*] For more information, see EBRD publications.

could lead to business closings. In this context it is worth mentioning what Lady Margaret Thatcher wrote in her memoirs:* "The difference between the public and the private sector was that the private sector was controlled by the government and the public sector wasn't controlled by anyone."

e) The state can require business licenses and permits only when the object of the business is a matter of public interest. Even under these circumstances there should be penalties for an unjustified delay in the issuance of such licenses. In this respect, as in others, special attentions should be paid to fight corruption and bureaucratic attitudes that can stifle private initiative.

The issue of control as an attribute of private property is also of great importance and should be analyzed from several different angles. First, to fully exercise his right to ownership the owner must have all legal or any other means to control his property (business of any kind) and should not have to share this right except when it is in his interest to do so. It is very important to know exactly the limits to which the right of private property, or of the private capital invested in a business, can be exercised, especially in the case where a significant number of shares have already been distributed to the employees and to the previous management of that business. A potential domestic or foreign investor should not have to fear that his management could be undermined or paralyzed by the sometimes divergent interests of the employees or by the previous management of that company, or by certain arbitrary measures taken by the government.

Secondly, it is important that the private investor who decided to acquire an enterprise for business purposes should be entitled to audit the components of the balance sheet on which the acquisition offer is based to verify the physical inventory that is to become his property and to be free to use any means to liquidate any possible discrepancies before actually taking over the enterprise. In other

---

* *The Downing Street Years* (Harper Collins Publishers, 1993), p. 6; Mrs. Thatcher is citing Mr. Arthur Shenfield.

words, he should be free to withdraw his offer if the initial conditions have not been met.

Provisions should also exist for cases where there are different claims to the same property. This happens often when the dispute involves the right to ownership of the land on which the enterprise of the potential new owner is built. In this case, the lease of the land should be worded in a way which does not needlessly impede the activity of the new owner. When a conflict cannot be avoided, a long-term lease or a joint venture with the owner of the land is preferable both for the government (when it owns the land) and for the investor.

To avoid disputes with other claimants and to speed the privatization process it is generally preferable to solve, in one way or another, the claims on nationalized property before its auctioning. Also, the government should first liquidate the companies which it intends to sell and to assume the obligation to cover their debts, so that the new buyer would take over a business free of any liabilities (except in regards to the land). It is desirable that once the private property has been instituted, the public sector should be implicated as little as possible in the work of the private sector. This should be specified in the provisions of the law.

Finally, there should be a preferential policy for the private entrepreneurs who are nationals of the given country. To avoid nationalistic resentment it is advisable that the first auctioning of a property should give priority to the citizens of that country. When an enterprise is auctioned, priority should be given to its employees; whenever possible a discount should be offered not only in appreciation for their loyalty, but also to encourage interest-sharing in the new private enterprise. The same criteria should be used when payment in installments is accepted. However, in an inflationary environment the installments should be indexed to the rate of inflation in order to preserve the initial value of the enterprise; this would also accelerate the privatization process for the buyer.

As previously stated, a clear specification of the rights of the owner should go hand in hand with an equally clear delineation of his obligations, deriving from his relations with third parties, especially with the government, not as a former owner but as a representative of community interests. As a representative of its citizens, the government also has the duty to control the way in which the right of ownership is exercised (within the limits mentioned at the beginning of this chapter). By relations with third parties we also have in mind the relations of the owner of an enterprise with his business partners (suppliers or clients) regarding his contractual obligations and his relations with banks or financial institutions which are entitled to exercise a rigorous financial control over the way he uses their financial resources, temporarily lent to him.

Mindful of the general interests, the government is entitled to modify fiscal legislation and the provisions of the budget which could lead to changes in income taxes or to introduce taxes to prevent speculative tendencies, to enact anti-trust legislation or to apply bankruptcy law as a penalty for the improper use of the right to ownership to the detriment of the interest of other owners.

When the government exercises these rights with respect to the regulation of private property, it is very important that it acts with competence, honesty and a desire to assist the private sector. Experience shows that in the former communist countries this is a major issue, not only because the bureaucracy is not ready for this new role, but also because of undesirable political pressures and insufficient compensation for the employees in the public sector. The parallel existence of the private sector, where employees are paid a higher salary, stimulates corruption, while the legislation to prevent such abuses is not always applied. This is why it is best not to hold onto the illusion that private property and the existence of a free market will automatically insure the success of reform. The human factor plays a major role in the fate of reform.

Thus is it not surprising that, when mentioning these issues, Western analysts of the transition process in the former communist countries stress the need for precise rules of conduct for the managers of public enterprises. These rules are needed because, as opposed to how things were in the past, managers are inevitably competing with their peers in the private sector. Therefore their responsibilities, expected rewards, and the risk of being replaced for unsatisfactory performance need to be clearly spelled out. The regulations should expressly specify the penalties for abuse of power. They should emphasize the need to use information in the interests of the enterprise for which the manager works and not for his personal goals, the need to avoid conflicts of interest that would raise doubts regarding a manager's honesty, as well introduce incentives to accept calculated risks inherent to business activity.

The managers of public enterprises should also have a stake in the price of the shares of their enterprise traded on the stock exchange; they should keep an eye open for innovations, be loyal to their company and fair to other companies.

Our intention here was to stress the Western view about the need for transparency in the private sector. These are just some general points which should suggest the type of issues encountered in this period.

The following table (**Table 4**) attempts to provide a general picture of the development of the private sector in the economies of some former communist countries. Caution should be exercised in the use of the figures, as they are based on different sources: methods of record-keeping, integration and reporting may vary according to different interpretations in the given countries.

The next table (**Table 5**), designed by the author, reflects the number and proportion of people involved in the private sector in Romania in 1992. The figures are based on data in Romania's *Statistical Yearbook* for 1993, pp. 110, 111, and 115.

## TABLE 4
### THE WEIGHT OF THE PRIVATE SECTOR
### IN THE TOTAL GDP*

#### National Statistics

|  | 1989 | 1990 | 1991 | 1992 |
|---|---|---|---|---|
| Bulgaria | 7.2 | 9.5 | 11.9 | 15.6 |
| Czechoslovakia | 4.1 | 5.3 | 8.1 | --- |
| Poland** |  | (28.6) |  |  |
| Romania | 13.0 | 16.4 | 21.0 | 25.6 |
| Hungary (1) | 24.4 | --- | 27.0 | --- |

#### The Vienna Institute For Comparative Economic Studies

|  | 1989 | 1990 | 1991 | 1992 |
|---|---|---|---|---|
| Bulgaria | --- | --- | 5-18 | 5-18 |
| Czechoslovakia | --- | --- | 10 | 20 |
| Poland** |  | (30.9) |  |  |
| Romania | --- | --- | --- | --- |
| Hungary (1) | --- | 18.0 | 28.0 | 33.0 |

#### The UN Economic Commission For Europe

|  | 1989 | 1990 | 1991 | 1992 |
|---|---|---|---|---|
| Bulgaria | --- | --- | 5 | 10 |
| Czechoslovakia | 4.1 | 5.2 | 9.3 | 20 |
| Poland** | (42.1) |  | (45.0-50.0) |  |
| Romania | --- | --- | --- | 26 |
| Hungary (1) | --- | 10.0 | 27.0 | 35.0 |
| Hungary (2) | --- | 13.0 | 13.6 | 25.0 |

Hungary (1) - Data of the Ministry of Finance based on tax receipts
Hungary (2) - Data of the Central Statistical Office based on the size of
      the labor force

\* Published in "Economic Review," Annual Economic Outlook, Sept.
  1993, p. 64.
\*\* The figures are in brackets as they also include cooperatives.

## TABLE 5

**THE NUMBER AND PROPORTION OF PEOPLE
INVOLVED IN THE PRIVATE SECTOR IN 1992**

|  | No. of households | No. of people in households |
|---|---|---|
| **Total** | 7,288,676 | 22,385,707 |
| of which in private sector: **Head of households** |  |  |
| - Independent businessmen | 25,302 | 84,163 |
| - Individual farmers | 489,764 | 1,592,745 |
| - Members of an agricultural, probably private, association | 83,219 | 271,066 |
| - Private artisans and merchants | 44,388 | 171,289 |
| **Subtotal** | 642,673 | 2,119,263 |
| % of private sector households in the total number of house- holds | 8.8% |  |
| % of people in the private sector in the total household popula- tion (July 1, 1992 census) |  | 9.3% |
| % of active population in the private sector in the total active population |  | 20.3% |

The actual figures could be higher, as the above-figures do not include the employees in the private sector, but they could also be lower, if all the persons in the household do not work in the private sector, as is assumed in the Table 5.

# IV

## BASIC ISSUES CONCERNING THE ACCELERATION OF PRIVATIZATION

### A. THE PROS AND CONS OF PRIVATIZATION

Perhaps to some, the very choice of this subtitle might seem peculiar. We believe, however, that it clearly expresses the position of many governments in ex-communist countries. Stating this, we make reference not only to those who, for their own reasons, look upon privatization unfavorably, but more so to privatization advocates acting against it.

In February 1990, shortly after the upheaval in Central and Eastern Europe, the author toured most of the countries in the region as a representative of the Republic National Bank of New York. As such, he took part in the Prague conference on the economic transition period in the ex-communist countries and used this opportunity to visit Romania. After anticipating his visit for so long, the painful reality caught him unprepared.[*]

Realizing the austerity facing Romanians, the author had tried, as much as he could, to lend a helping hand. According to his proposal, the Romanian American Chamber of Commerce[†] was established in New York in 1990. He also proposed, unsuccessfully however, the creation of a bank called the "Youth's Bank." Within the same context, the author had discussions with various politicians on the issue of privatizing and attracting foreign capital. Towards the end of the same year, he organized a seminar in Bucharest on this topic. In conversations on privatization issues with a leading Parliamentary official, he was completely taken aback by the position of

---

[*] I left Romania in 1975, a time when many of my friends in Bucharest deemed the situation acceptable. To me, things looked grim even at that time, even though I could hardly fathom how much worse it could get. Upon return, all memories were shattered. The house I grew up in had been demolished and most of my friends had disappeared or were scattered all over the world.

[†] The Romanian American Chamber of Commerce was established in 1990 in New York. Towards the end of 1992, I resigned from my position as president because of some fundamental differences with its Chairman. For details please see the article "A Spectacular Resignation," *Romania Libera*, March 26, 1993.

his interlocutor, later echoed by the slogan used in the Romanian media: "this country is not for sale." His surprise was triggered not only by the fact that officials resorted to an outmoded axiom, at a time when the world economy was based on interdependent relationships, but more so by the intent to initiate a climate of suspicion for both locals and potential foreign investors in a country recently liberated from a dictatorial system that had isolated her from the international economic circuit.

Such a slogan made the author take advantage of this meeting to relay to his interlocutor a story that created much excitement in New York. At about that time, or perhaps earlier, Japan, while showing a huge surplus in its balance of trade with the United States, went on a shopping spree of American firms and properties. Many began to reckon how long it would take before the entire New York financial center would be totally "conquered," without a single bullet being fired. A very heated debate was caused by the acquisition of an important New York building – in a way the symbol of American capitalism – namely, the Rockefeller Center, situated in the heart of an exclusive Manhattan area.

Rockefeller Center, which is an enormous edifice, suffered no harm as a result of its buy-out. The building could not be shipped to Japan and Americans continue to enjoy the benefits of this complex which includes an excellent skating rink and world-famous restaurants. All offices located in the building, many of which house financial companies competing with the Japanese, continued their activities unencumbered. On the other hand, New York real estate started to feel the effects of a prolonged recession. We cannot remember the exact dollar amount paid by the Japanese for acquiring the Rockefeller Center, but as the recession continued, its value diminished considerably. Maintenance expenses for such a huge compound became a serious issue and the Japanese decided, after a time, to sell it at a loss. In fact, it would come as no surprise that the new buyers are the original landlords. Similar events took place in Boston. An example is the huge Wang Laboratories conglomerate which cost millions of dollars and was sold for a only few hundred thousand. The moral of these stories is that in a world in which the free market economy is working beyond national boundaries, a slogan such as "This country is not for sale" is totally irrelevant, except, perhaps, for a small group of extreme nationalists.*

The pressures exerted by the extreme right, although a serious diversion, represent only one, and not a very significant, aspect of the privatization issue. The real question resides in its modes of implementation given the fact that only four years ago Romania had an economic structure defined as monopolistic state capitalism (see Chapter I).

In contrast to Western privatization which, to make use of a terminology used in sports, took place on its own "playing field" and made the "local team" feel reassured, the very foundations needed to enable this process were missing in ex-communist countries. In an already complicated equation, the transition from a centrally planned economy to a market economy introduced a new element – privatization – which also became its main unknown factor.

It is also worth mentioning the fact that in ex-communist countries, privatization has to encompass not only one large company or sector, but huge spheres of the national economy, in fact the overwhelming majority of national assets. It is, therefore, extremely broad in area and depth. In addition, this whole process has to be accomplished in a relatively short historical period.

Our experience points to the fact that there are various methods for solving this issue. The classical approach would assume:

a) the presence of a large market for domestic capital or the creation, over the shortest possible period of time, of all of its necessary ingredients, through a banking system complemented by:

b) an influx of foreign capital, resulting from direct investments, joint ventures, etc., or foreign credits and financing through international commercial banks. This course would be similar to the general pattern of privatization followed by capitalist countries, irrespective of their level of development.

---

* We cannot ignore the fact that as long as poverty, starvation, obscurantism and fanaticism prevail, extreme right wing ideas continue to find favorable ground. Although education and training have spread considerably, their impact is limited by austere circumstances.

It is evident that the environment of post-1989 Romania made this route impossible, mainly because of the absence of a domestic capital market. Moreover, even though foreign debts did not burden the country, bureaucracy, corruption and incompetence kept foreign investors away.

After 1989, another possible course appeared under the sponsorship of international financial organizations such as the International Monetary Fund, the World Bank, the European Bank for Reconstruction and Development, etc. In essence, this course, which is a substitute for a domestic capital market, represents a partial redistribution of national wealth to the population, either for free or in exchange for a symbolic payment.

There is a fundamental difference between these two courses in creating a domestic capital market. The former was the result of a historical process, a natural evolution that created not only the economic and financial infrastructure for development, but also an adequate psychological climate for accepting the criteria of both risk and profit. It also entailed very limited state intervention. The latter approach introduces an artificial pattern, totally opposed to the prior structure in the ex-communist countries, ignoring the psychological factor in the evolution of the economic process and giving the state a preponderant role. It appears that, as in any artificial transplant, an adverse reaction comes naturally under such circumstances, and the only question is how to reduce and gradually eliminate its impact. Both the Romanian experience and that of other ex-communist countries underline that, at least thus far, we are witnessing the beginning of this process. The very definition of privatization is in the process of gestation, while the state, by its very nature and especially as a result of its previous role, acts as a brake instead of a stimulant of creativity.

It becomes clearer that the representatives of the above-mentioned international financial institutions, unfamiliar with the socio-economic reality of ex-communist countries and the impact of half a century of dictatorship, have failed in setting up an adequate model for the transition period. Ignored was the fact that the so-called "socialism" had the characteristics of a primitive monopolistic state capitalism that had to be abolished and replaced with a competitive capitalism, able to hold out on its own and not be carried on the back of the state apparatus.

In fact, the model of freely redistributing part of the national wealth raises many questions related to the degree in which it can substitute for the emergence of a real capital market, as well as to the duration of transition. The manner in which this redistribution is proposed to take place – which theoretically ought to increase the purchasing power of the population – only gives rise to the <u>illusion of enrichment</u> and is debatable in terms of financial consistency, its material coverage, and the inflationary potential that can be aroused.

Another course to privatization, which seems to be more adequate to the specific economic conditions in Romania, is – in the author's opinion – to use, in a skillful way, the domestic resources, for the time being mostly agricultural, through rational stimulants of the mechanisms of market economy (such as price, interest, profit, credit, etc.). We will clarify this topic in the next chapter.

Privatization in both Western and ex-communist countries has a number of common objectives:

- to free up funds from the national budget previously designed to subsidize unprofitable companies and thus reduce the deficit;
- to allow the new owners to introduce superior technological means for increasing productivity and, hence, output;
- to create the prerequisites for reducing costs and increasing profits and competitiveness;
- to become a supplementary source of budgetary revenue.

In addition to these factors, the impact of privatization in ex-communist countries is considerably greater due to the following:

- it represents the only solution for creating and developing a private economic sector indispensable in a market economy;
- it reduces the unemployment resulting from the closure of distressed state companies;
- it allows a fundamental redirection of agriculture and the modern restructuring of industry;
- it attracts foreign capital to direct investments and joint ventures;

- it channels toward production resources made temporarily available in the banking system and stimulates the economy as a whole;
- it allows the establishment and expansion of a broad social safety net, a basic element of the reform process as a whole.

Almost five years ago, during an interview granted to *Libertatea*, a Romanian daily, and published on June 5-6, 1991, the author referred to the draft law on privatization, warning against state involvement and centralization, which were apparent in the draft. He advanced the idea of allowing an evolution in accord with the requirements of the emerging market economy.

Within this context, the author criticized the trend towards creating bureaucratic structures, the interference that could occur between these structures and the independent management of companies, and resulting from this interference, the impairment of the effect on supply and demand which in turn could complicate both small and large scale privatization. He also mentioned that these new structures, set at the crossroads between holders of certificates of ownership and the company itself, might lead to technical problems having undesirable practical consequences on the process of converting these certificates into shares, as well as on the decision as how to utilize the dividends. Finally, he noted that the existence and functioning of these new structures can negatively influence the decision of foreign investors to participate in the privatization process in Romania.

During the same interview the author emphasized the debatable character of the balance sheet data used in evaluating the companies to be privatized, the absence in the draft law of stipulations relating to priority directions to be considered in this undertaking, as well as the omission of any reference to areas of the Romanian economy looking for foreign capital.

Another flaw of the draft law was the fact that it did not spell out stimulating means for attracting the excess cash of the market to be used in financing small scale privatization, nor the procedures for establishing and expanding the capital market for large scale privatization. Finally, the draft law made no reference to the essential role of the banking sector in implementing privatization or the direct participation of trade unions in facilitating this process.

A separate segment of the interview addressed with some reservations regarding the issue of "free distribution" in accelerating the privatization process. During the interview, the author tried to outline his own views and proposals concerning privatization in an ex-communist country committed to democratic government. These proposals were made at the beginning of June 1991, and those who intend to make a comparison with the text that follows will notice that all recent changes are insignificant, and that the recommendations are even more valid today, four years after Law 58/1991 was signed.

Within this context we proposed to create a Privatization Committee (which can be called today the General Privatization Committee, or GPC for short) as a <u>temporary</u> institution, led by a <u>trilateral commission</u> which would reflect the present economic structure: <u>state</u> representatives, designated by the executive branch with the accord of the legislative branch, representatives of <u>company</u> management (we have in mind representatives of those companies marked for privatization, and who will be replaced in this Committee by a different set of managers, once the companies have been privatized), and representatives of the <u>trade unions</u> of the companies to be privatized at a given moment. Therefore, while the structure of the Committee remains the same, the actors change, reflecting the different companies to be privatized.

Trade union representatives have a significant political and economic role in the privatization process. In addition to underlining the democratic character of this process, their inclusion in the process sets guarantees for union members and can play an important part in ensuring the establishment of a policy of social protection, in avoiding strikes, in defining their position in relation not only with the potential employers, but also with the trade unions of competitor companies, and the degree to which they can support the demands of other trade unions.

The GPC should have an independent character – not as a government entity – and should bring forward the <u>common</u> preoccupations of the three groups responsible for ensuring the establishment of a private sector by consensus.

It is worth mentioning that, according to this proposal, only a very limited number of the members of this committee would be permanent salaried personnel, while the rest is assigned as previously described.

Further, the above committee was to be divided into two distinct components in charge of small and large scale privatization and subsequently subdivided into specialized groups (branches and sub-branches of the economy) mirroring the composition of the GPC. The issue of employment expenses for component and group subdivisions has to be treated in the same manner as the case of the GPC, i.e., minimal personnel on the payroll.

This composition (a trilateral committee at every level) ensures the transparency needed for the entire operation and enables flexibility, a characteristic indispensable to this process.

In the absence of useless bureaucratic structures, each specialized component and group can function within the framework established by the GPC, setting, for their limited existence, their own agenda and budgets with revenues and expenses operated by commercial banks organized or adapted for this purpose. As a consequence, the privatization process will be supported by the banking system, the only entity capable of mobilizing and productively utilizing the financial resources resulting from this vast undertaking, as well as from other domestic and international economic and financial operations.

Finally, if certificates of ownership are issued, they should be automatically, or in the shortest possible period of time, assimilated with the shares of the respective companies, skipping a state-controlled bureaucratic conversion period. This transfer should take place within the system of a free market through brokerage houses or a banking system adapted for this purpose. The market, through supply and demand, will inform economic agents (initially through the GPC and its sub-divisions) of the fluctuation of these financial instruments to allow the holders of Certificates of Ownership to make a choice.

Official publications show that a number of suggestions made by the author as part of "General Scheme" of 1990 (see Addendum 2), as well as some made during the interview of 1991, have materialized. Thus, commercial companies were divided into three groups*: small-sized companies (assets under 500 million lei, and less than 500 employees) – approximately 2,600 units – which should

---

* According the *Romanian Economic Newsletter*, July-Sept. 1993, p. 4, on December 31, 1992, there were 6291 commercial companies designated for privatization, with a total capital of 9 trillion lei, with 300 trillion in business transactions and employing about 1/3 of the entire labor force.

be rapidly privatized; medium-sized companies (assets of less than 3 billion lei, and less than 3,000 employees) – approximately 2,900 units – which will be authorized by the Private Ownership Fund (POF) to initiate the privatization process with the exception of those connected to large companies or companies needed for strategic considerations. In case of the large state companies (assets over 3 billion lei and over 3,000 employees) – approximately 800 units – privatization is to be made following feasibility studies, organizational restructuring, etc., on a case by case basis. The State Ownership Fund (SOF) has the responsibility to advance annual proposals to Parliament regarding its privatization program. This last group will be the subject of a strategic analysis based on a selective restructuring policy and economic priority (comparative advantage in terms of exports, considerations related to raw material, labor force, etc.).

Within this context, the following areas will be given first consideration: the agricultural and food sectors, commerce, tourism, textiles and garments, leather, footwear, wood processing, transportation, construction and building materials. Moreover, each Fund, according to these regulations, will develop its own strategy and budget and avoid bureaucratic entanglements by contacting directly domestic or foreign companies in relation to the privatization process. We believe that the *Monitorul Oficial* (Official Journal) will be instrumental in informing the economic agents on the process of privatizing.

We welcome these measures, which take partial heed of our critique and the above-mentioned proposals. However, other important critiques and proposals have been ignored. We refer mainly to the management of these Funds which makes them state-dependent, leaves out trade union representatives, neglects the role of the banking sector, etc. The institutions responsible for privatization, as created by Law 58/1991, do not take into account changes that have taken place in the economy over these last few years and should be restructured to reflect the new conditions. We believe that such modifications would draw them closer to the models envisioned in our proposals.

## B. PRIVATE OWNERSHIP FUND AND TO WHOM THE CERTIFICATES OF OWNERSHIP BELONG

We would like to begin by referring to the role and place of the Private Ownership Fund (POF) as being most constantly in the public eye and having to play a significant part in the future. (We should emphasize the fact that our analysis of the structure of the Private Ownership Fund and its functions was made prior to the publication, in June 1995, of the government program on accelerating the privatization process. We believe, however, that it is needed, in particular for the Western reader unfamiliar with the situation in Romania.)*

In agreement with the provisions of Law 58/1991 on privatizing commercial companies, the POF functions within the framework of the Statute of the National Agency for the Privatization and Development of Small and Medium Sized Companies. Our remarks refer, therefore, to the Statute. Reading this normative act we are surprised by the place occupied by the Private Ownership Fund within the framework of the privatization process. It follows that the Private Ownership Fund concomitantly performs several functions:

a) as a large commercial company;
b) issuer of certificates of ownership to Romanian citizens, in compliance with Law 58/1991;
c) manager of certificates of ownership;
d) brokerage services, etc.

Undoubtedly, these functions are not incompatible and can be performed by one independent economic agent. They are, however, contrary to the transient nature of the Private Ownership Fund and its role as state representative.

In 1994, when this book was written for the Romanian audience, in the author's opinion, POF should have finalized the transfer of certificates of ownership to the population and ceased to exist as a state enterprise. As soon as this transfer is completed, the holders of certificates of ownership should become economically independent of the Private Ownership Fund, whose activity should be limited only:

---

* According to the information we have, a new structure for the Private Ownership Fund was not implemented in 1995.

a) to manage certificates of ownership (which belong to
their holders);
b) to perform brokerage activities with these certificates as
ordered by certificate holders.

Under these circumstances, the Private Ownership Fund
cannot perform as a commercial company, as it *does not hold* any
shares (the initial 30% of shares allotted to it have been transferred
to Certificate of Ownership holders). It cannot maximize profits and
capitalize the gains of companies that should perform independently;
it should not have any role in distributing the dividends of such
companies or in their investment policy, and it should not take any
part which could influence the freedom of the respective companies.

Unfortunately this was not the case. The Private Ownership
Fund was involved – and even in 1995 it has been continuously
involved – in most important financial and business decisions of these
companies.

The Statute stipulates repeatedly that the certificates of ownership are bearer titles (art 3.1), that any ownership certificate holder
is its legal owner (art. 3.7), thus clarifying for us who has the ownership title. Under these circumstances, how can the same certificates
of ownership be the stock of the Private Ownership Fund (art. 2.2)?
In other words, if the ownership certificate holders are the owners
of the Private Ownership Fund stock, they should manage the Private
Ownership Fund activity rather than leave it to organizations designated by the state.

If the ownership certificate holder is the real owner of this
document, how can the Private Ownership Fund have the right to
decide on the procedures for exchanging them for shares, in terms of
numbers and circumstances allowing this exchange, on the utilization
of dividends, on controlling this activity, etc.? The total dependence
of the ownership certificate holder on the Private Ownership Fund,
in spite of the fact that he is the owner, is detailed in Art. 5.1 of the
Statute, which stipulates that "possession of an ownership certificate
assumes a <u>complete and unreserved</u> acceptance of the Private Ownership Fund Statute as the issuer of ownership certificates" (my
emphasis – DG).

In fact, this is a very good example of the ambiguous nature of
how the right to private ownership is defined in the Romanian
legislation. The same ambiguity characterizes the terms of exchang-

ing certificates of ownership for shares, with the Private Ownership Fund controlling the entire operation, The law superposes the "owner" with the "owner representative" giving the POF decision making powers, in spite of the fact that the certificates of ownership now belong to their holders.

If the Private Ownership Fund can assume its real role within the private sector rather than being a state organization, huge amounts of money, currently subsidized by the government, could become available and be used for accelerating privatization.

Until that time, the role of the Private Ownership Fund should be to manage certificates of ownership on behalf of and at the request of those owners who have not yet taken possession of their certificates. This would entail such transactions as purchases, sales, transfers from one fund to another, as well as the temporary deposit of the certificates until their real owners petition them. The Fund cannot, thus, substitute for the real owners. These functions should be performed by the Private Ownership Fund in the same way as other brokers, without bureaucratic obstacles or prior approvals at various levels.

Undoubtedly, the POF should receive a commission for brokering on behalf of the owners (and this should also constitute its future function). Utilizing the banking system, the Private Ownership Fund should use this resource for creating its own social stock which, as shown further, could be multiplied in different ways. Appointments in the management of the Private Ownership Fund should not be made by the executive branch. In order to ensure transparency in its activity, the POF should attract personalities from the field of science, education, culture, etc., known for their honesty and competence.

Such a structure, and its complete integration with the private sector, could bring about the prerequisites for performing its temporary function of periodically establishing the market value of these certificates, a function that should be passed on to the free market as soon as possible.

The Private Ownership Fund, designated in its entirety by the executive branch, functions alongside with the National Agency for Privatization, the National Agency for Privatizing and Developing Small and Medium Sized Companies, The National Agency for Ownership Titles, and we are not sure if the list ends here. In 1995, we read about the establishment of a new commission, the Agency for Industrial Restructuring. It is our belief that increasing the number of agencies will not lead to an acceleration of the privatization process, but will create more bureaucratic structures. If this newly created agency is indeed needed, we were unable to find any mention of reducing the number of personnel or savings resulting from improving its organizational system, etc.

In any capitalist country, privatization relies on the banking system, in particular investment banks, on pension funds and a network of stock brokers. These institutions allow the formation of large financial funds that can assist future private investors in the privatization process. Our proposal – that the certificates of ownership should be automatically assimilated with the shares – aims at the formation of a secondary capital market, the development of financial institutions and the acceleration of the privatization process.

Private Ownership Funds must play a very important role in creating a secondary capital market. Such a role entails initiative, risk taking and financial creativity to the end of attracting domestic and international capital. It must abandon its bureaucratic functions and become a fundamental instrument of the free market. It should have the right to use shares and bonds on the stock market (their acceptance is subject to strict regulations) and to constitute them into an active collateral used to solicit bank credits and preferential interest rates when they are used for accelerating privatization and in general the development of a productive private sector. Also, the Private Ownership Fund should introduce mutual funds which include shares and bonds classified according to different criteria in relation to consumer requirements (for growth, for dividends, for growth and dividends combined from various branches of the economy, etc.), thus diminishing the risk of investors.

As mutual funds are popular in the United State in particular, and the West in general, attracting the majority of private investors as well as many institutions, a diversified portfolio under the conditions of a stabilized economy will become an interesting investment for Western mutual fund managers. They will be tempted to include such shares in their portfolio, bringing them to the attention of the international financial market.

Converting the POF into investments funds, similar to mutual funds in the USA, would take a longer period of time. This cannot be done overnight. Most likely, this institution will increase considerably to gradually include parts of the State Ownership Fund.

Consequently, its reorganization should rely on a detailed analysis of the balance sheets of companies with shares to be traded and should scrutinize the macroeconomic conditions affecting the evolution of the GNP, interest rates, unemployment, credit policy, etc.

As is probably known, circumstances are slightly more favorable to small privatization; large privatization faces many difficulties, among them the limited participation of foreign investments.*

Although the issue of the State Ownership Fund will be tangential approached in Chapter V, we should anticipate an incomplete analysis due to our lack of information.

## C. DIFFERENCES BETWEEN OUR PROPOSALS AND THE GOVERNMENT PROGRAM

Adam Smith and David Ricardo would consider very strange, and completely alien to their way of thinking, the idea of freely distributing a portion of the assets (or as some may desire, of the entire assets) of an company or the national wealth to those who actively participated in its creation – hence, independent of the free market. It is a well known fact that the Ricardian system of income distribution (land rent—profit—salary) excluded the idea of free distribution. In fact, aside from land reforms brought about by different considerations, Western economists in more recent times did not view free distribution as an economic criterion. Quite the contrary, they deemed it as undermining the economic initiative for raising profits, the main production incentive in a market economy.

In consequence, the idea of free distribution as an economic factor has a very short history, emerging after the collapse of the totalitarian regime in ex-communist countries. Viewed from a moral point of view, the entire population and not only the active group, with the exception of the former nomenclature, should be compensated for the physical and material sufferings imposed by the former communist regimes. Justice, however, should be brought from a different direction that would not affect economic development. We agree that the population and not the state should be the main

---

* In June 1995, foreign investments totaled $1.37 billion (between January and June 1995 the growth was approximately $99 million – *Romanian Economic Newsletter*, July-September, 1995, vol. 5, no. 2, page 4.

beneficiary of de-nationalization. Nevertheless, to achieve this goal a different pattern should be used, as shown later. In fact, not all neighboring countries introduced the idea of free distribution in the privatization process. It is not evident that it was used in Hungary and we do not have information on Bulgaria. In 1991, in Czechoslovakia, the population had to pay the symbolic price of $35 for a voucher.

These facts do not represent the main arguments in our debate. The most important question refers to the practical functioning of the program of certificates of ownership and its many restrictions in an emerging free market economy.

In Romania, under the current legislation, 30% of the capital of privatized or to be privatized companies will be distributed free of charge to the population. We are not debating now the criteria of the distribution itself, the number of coupons given to each person, or the way of evaluating these documents. Moreover, we do not have any information related to reparations to be paid to former company owners or if nationalized companies will be returned to them. Therefore, we intend to refer only to the effects of free distribution and the problems it raises, as presented in 1990.* To this we will add a number of more recent details.

Here is a list of problems, not given in order of importance:

1. Certificate holders, assuming that they have also the coupons at this time, will be able to:

   a) keep them and receive dividends from the Private Ownership Fund and/or become Private Ownership Fund shareholders, when the Private Ownership Fund becomes a mutual fund;
   b) keep them and exchange them for shares of a given company when it is privatized;
   c) trade them on the free market. (This last option is to be clarified by the Government.)

In the case where certificate holders opt to keep them, in a free market their value can increase or diminish. If they consider

---

* This viewpoint was published in the Romanian newspaper *Economistul*, January 15-17, 1991.

this option, they will have to make an uninformed decision as there are no financial institutions to assist them at this time, and stock brokers question the "market value" established by the Private Ownership Fund.*

Certificate holders also face another risk: the large majority of privatized companies have inexperienced managers, who will merely try to survive during these first years, under the circumstances of real competition. Along these lines, it is well known that in the United States almost 50% of bankruptcies are small and medium-sized companies with 1-3 years on the market, in spite of the fact that people have more experience and risk their own money. As a result – at least in the first years – the probability of depreciation is higher than that of appreciation, with very few exceptions. Facing this risk, most certificate holders will try to sell them as soon as possible and, with supply higher than demand, the price will probably drop dramatically.†

In the absence of an organized mechanism consisting of stock brokers or private banks that will assume part of this risk, we will witness a stock market crash. Foreign investors will not rush to buy under such circumstances. In fact, it appears that foreign investors are out of the competition. We believe that the possibility of a market crash was not examined in the current program.**

2. Let us assume, no matter how absurd this will appear given the circumstances of a market economy and a relatively high inflation, that the value of stock will remain unchanged. Even if we accept this foolish hypothesis, the value of the shares distributed to the population cannot stimulate future material growth. This value represents only the monetary expression of already created goods which will pass – due to this redistribution – from the state to the population, without contributing anything to the size of the national wealth and

---

* See "SERCA SA questions the Private Ownership Fund Monopoly Position," published in the daily newspaper *Romania Libera*, January 1994.
† In our assumptions we did not take into account the inflation factor which acts adversely on the shares' value (and other kinds of financial instruments).
** In 1994, the stock of a large Russian company, MMM, dropped 50% in one day. The decline continued for the next several days. Shareholders panicked and started to sell. As a result, the value of the stock plummeted from $55 to approximately 50 cents.

hence, to the further development of economy. Therefore, new companies cannot be created with certificates of ownership because they do not generate fresh capital. It is also impossible to make needed imports using certificates of ownership.

We estimate that those advancing the idea of free distribution were interested in attracting the masses thus making them more determined to increase production and productivity. Nevertheless, good intentions do not make up for the current lack of raw materials, modern equipment, etc.

We witness in reverse the old illusion of 1948 when almost the entire economy was nationalized and everybody became, according to the communist doctrine an "owner." Free distribution has never been an economic incentive. It triggers <u>waste and lack of responsibility</u>.

3. The number of future ownership certificate holders was estimated at 15.5 million (on December 31, 1991). They will not be able to directly control the activity of approximately 6,000 companies, characterized previously in relation to the number of employees and asset value. Direct control is impossible as the ownership certificate holders and future shareholders are spread all over the country. Thus, the Board of Directors of these companies will be the decision makers. The 15.5 million people will be owners by proxy. This would not be a concern if the members of these Boards are familiar with a market economy, but this is not the case. As a result, if the company goes bankrupt, the shareholders will lose everything.

In the United States, investors are very cautious. They choose a broker. Brokerage houses have research departments specialized in studying the domestic and international market, in making economic and financial forecasts, in anticipating different possible scenarios for political changes and their impact on the stock market, in preparing models accordingly, etc. Brokerage houses have just emerged in Romania. They need time to gain experience and avoid unacceptable risks for their investors. In the meanwhile, confusion and uncertainty prevail regarding the decision to buy or sell certificates of ownership coupons or shares.

4. No attempt was made to relate the free distribution of certificates of ownership to a program aimed at voluntarily attracting excess cash from the market and thus eliminating a strong inflationary

element. The free distribution of certificates of ownership could have been paralleled by other financial instruments offered to the population. We will deal with this problem later on.

The free distribution of certificates of ownership entails the potential risk of a sudden, and given the conditions of a free market, even out of control, increase in the amount of excess cash that cannot be channeled towards production due to the lack of a financial market capable of absorbing it. This could further amplify an inflationary climate.

5. Another problem related to the free distribution of certificates of ownership is the need for technological modernization and economic restructuring possible by correcting the present gaps. This can only be accomplished by attracting foreign capital. The free distribution of certificates of ownership, soon to become shares, will probably have a negative effect on foreign investors as it contradicts the common sense of the Western businessman. Potential foreign investors will be reluctant to buy these shares even when prices drop. They will need guarantees that the issuer is legitimate and they will not be treated as outsiders by the "insiders" in this process, or be denied the control to which they are entitled in their capacity of co-investors.

The above analysis and critique represent personal opinions, as presented in 1990's seminar, when a decision had to be made regarding free distribution. We do not know if these facts have been confirmed. We raised this issue not for a retrospective glance, but for preventing undesirable consequences.

The Law on accelerating the privatization process principally regulates these new financial instruments, namely the certificates of ownership and nominative coupons for privatization. This brings about the main distinctions between the program proposed by us and the government program.

A superficial reading reveals that both programs use similar concepts, such as the exchange of certificates of ownership for shares, modifying the role of the Private Ownership Fund, reviewing the legal framework, etc. Firstly, the author would like to mention that he submitted his proposals to the Editura Enciclopedica publishing house, in Bucharest, in *April 1994*. The government program was published in the Romanian media after several months. It is not impossible that during this period of time some of the ideas presented in the author's book had become known. Secondly, all similarities refer only to the object to be approached and not to the modality of our approach. Our viewpoints are completely different in this respect.

The government program, hoping to accelerate mass privatization and to offer the population a more attractive formula as compared to the disappointments since the Revolution, introduced, in addition to the certificate of ownership, a nominative coupon for privatization, which represents about 35 times the value of a certificate. The outcome cannot be ignored.

In compliance with official figures, at the end of 1990, approximately 15.5 million people had the right to receive a certificate of ownership. (This figure is probably slightly different now, as it includes those being 18 years of age at the end of 1995.) This number, multiplied by 900,000 lei per person results in the astronomical figure of 13.95 trillion lei. Converted to dollars at a rate of 1,800 lei to $1 (at the end of 1994), this represents $77.5 billion. In relation to the GNP of approximately $25.5 billion (22.76 million population x $1,120 GNP per inhabitant in 1993 – as published by the World Bank) we come to a figure 3 times larger that the entire GNP in 1993, and almost 16 times larger than the amount of total export in that year.

Such a huge figure could have grave inflationary consequences and unrealistically places Romania among the first countries in the world in terms of its stock market potential. Also Romania would appear as one of the most capital-oriented countries in the world because of its huge percentage of shareholders (converted coupons) as compared to its total population. Issuing these coupons (future shares) on an incipient financial market could also be a serious reason for concern in Romania, given the critical financial bottleneck existing in the economy and the large number of uncompetitive companies with large deficits.

Please do not forget that large scale privatization, regardless of the economic reasons behind it, is essentially a financial operation. It entails a significant financial transfer (not necessarily cash) and, given the environment of a free market, cannot be stopped through artificial administrative means without hurting the entire economic mechanism. Sooner or later the financial monetary circuit is positively or negatively influenced by the reaction of the capital market at that moment.

Undoubtedly, not all coupons will be exchanged for shares or for cash at the same time, but the psychological inflationary pressure on a free market economy has been created. Assuming that over a period of one year, only 1% of the population decides to do (and this is only a minimal figure): this translates to 139.5 billion lei* (155,000 x 900,000) or $775 million, almost 3.3% of the total GDP and about 15% of the total exports for 1993. These are very high numbers in relation to the current performance of the Romanian economy. Even accepting this possibility, the transfer of this minimal amount used for exchanging coupons for shares and converting them into financial instruments, would require a very long period of time, approximately 100 years.

Given the current situation of the Romanian economy, characterized by rudimentary competition and consumer goods prices much higher than the purchasing power of the population, the more rapid the creation of these new financial instruments, the higher the risk of inflation. Only the emergence of an active capital market and the presence of massive foreign credits and investments could correct this situation. But a capital market cannot be established overnight, and of so large proportion to fit the government program. In its absence, the inflationary trend not only continues, but is amplified.

We assume that in order to avoid this trap the government program stipulates that coupons holders are not be allowed - for the time being - to transact them on the market. (see Chapter 1, Art. 2, Par. 4). Hence, although the government declares that the mass privatization program targets the institution of the property right, it in fact sets restrictions regarding their transaction, and leaves unanswered the date when this operation will be possible. (Our work frequently mentions the lack of transparency in defining private property in Romania.) But in a free market economy, such infringements do not remove the danger of inflation. Quite the contrary, this violation of economic freedom brings this danger closer and it is only a question of *when*, and not *if*, it will materialized. Only a naive approach can ignore the impact of the psychological factor in the evolution of economic processes. Sooner or later, the

---

* Today this figure is probably much higher as the government raised the value of a coupon and the dollar exchange rate increased considerably.

coupon holders (and later shareholders) will inevitably be tempted to sell for cash and will find a way to go around the law. The cash thus obtained will not be used for the purchase of heavy industry goods, but, following a long period of deprivation, people will be inclined to satisfy their needs for consumer goods. However, there are not enough consumer goods to satisfy this increased purchasing power and hence, their artificially ballooned financial means will create the conditions for a rampant inflation.

The possible justification, that each company undergoing the privatization process will create its own material coverage is, in our opinion, utopian, because it ignores not only the relationship between the company output and the market demand for consumer goods, but also the precarious financial situation of such companies. In addition, the aggregate value of coupons (and later shares), distributed free of charge to the population – in other words, 13.95 trillion lei – represents only 30% of the assets of companies to be privatized. It follows that the total assets of these companies was approximately 46.5 trillion lei, a huge figure for the Romanian economy at the end of 1994.

Contemplating the fact that the envisioned financial instruments have no material coverage, the government program might consider a proposal advanced in this book: combining the conversion of certificates of ownership and nominative coupons for privatization with an *option* to buy government bonds that offer multiple benefits to their investors. In this case, why use this circumvented way that gave the illusion of enrichment which affected the credibility of the entire operation?

A different question is how would it be possible to convert in into shares (not to mention cash) the coupons issued by inefficient companies (many belonging to the heavy industry) or companies that may go bankrupt once government subsidies cease, or should be closed as a result of industrial restructuring?

The reasons stated above, while questioning the likelihood of mass privatization by the government program, may also explain its delayed adoption by the Romanian Parliament and leave room to future corrections.

In contrast with the government program, our program, starting from the Romanian economic situation in 1994 and taking into account the existence of the certificates of ownership, tries to lay out a framework free of inflationary trends. Thus, it formulates a set of measures that empower their rightful owners and converts them into genuine financial instruments.

With this purpose in mind, we anticipate a financial operation having the following main stages:

First, the state should offer to the new shareholder an <u>option</u> which, as outlined below, has multiple benefits. Thus, <u>concomitantly</u> with the conversion of certificates of ownership into shares by the Private Ownership Fund, the state should issue bonds with a term of, let's say, between a minimum of one year and a maximum of five years and having the following characteristics:

- interest is not taxable if the bonds are redeemed after five years, and is only partially taxable if redeemed sooner – that is after 1, 2, 3, or 4 years;
- a yearly interest should be paid to bond holders <u>in advance,</u> at the time of purchase, through Private Ownership Fund supplementary shares, estimated at market value minus a small commission (not higher than 3%) for performing this transaction;
- a <u>floating</u> interest rate will be used for paying bond holders, reflecting the rate of inflation and free market trends, thus allowing for an increase in the number of Private Ownership Fund supplementary shares to be paid under conditions of increased inflation;
- a sudden rise in inflation for considerations that cannot be anticipated will <u>automatically</u> entail an increase in the nominal value of bonds in relation to their <u>terms</u>[*];
- the bond interest rate should be relatively <u>lower</u> than that of commercial banks, taking into account the fact that it is non-taxable and offers special advantages including indexation;
- in addition, at the beginning of the year, the state will recommend bond holders to use the interest for <u>advanced</u> payment of their estimated taxes which, in this case, will enjoy, a <u>discount</u> of, let's say, 5%;

---

[*] The budget most probably will not be affected by this measure as the impact of inflation will be equal on incomes as well as expenditures.

- bonds having a maturity of at least 3 years will enter a drawing (beginning with the third year after purchase), organized in a pattern acceptable from budgetary considerations, so that some of the bond holders could get their nominal value in cash before the legal time for repayment.

Considering the many advantages of this new financial instrument, restrictions can be applied to insure its normal functioning. Thus, bond holders cannot ask the state to exchange their notes for cash before maturity without a high penalty; however, the notes can circulate on the secondary capital market (purchased by banks or brokers), and thus their nominal value will be updated through computations related to supply and demand.

How does the State benefit under these circumstances?

The state will absorb a large part of excess cash by selling bonds, while the benefits to consumers will not entail the use of cash or an increase in money supply; the amount possible to be absorbed could reach hundreds of billion lei, which would be utilized for a social safety net, the technological upgrade of productive sectors of the economy, etc.

Let's assume that only 25% (a low percentage in our opinion) of certificates of ownership holders, and respectively shareholders, are interested in purchasing state bonds in return for the benefits described above (e.g., paying taxes at discount rates, etc.) and will use only 25% of the value of certificates of ownership (turned shares) for this kind of option. In this hypothetical case, the State could acquire, considering the number of certificate of ownership holders (approximately 15.5 million on December 31, 1990) and the nominal value of the certificates of ownership at the end of 1993 (approximately 160,000 lei), approximately 170 billion lei at the beginning of the year rather than the end, untouched by the existing rate of inflation.

In addition, the immense amount thus absorbed will reduce inflationary pressures and its effect on the black market:

- the advance payment of an important part of taxes will, it is hoped, have favorable consequences on tax evasion and will cover a significant part of the interest paid with shares of the Private Ownership Fund, thus speeding up their sale and hence, privatization;

- if bond interest is not taxable (except at a given rate in relation to their maturity), the dividends from Private Ownership Fund supplementary shares will be treated as taxable income. This will represent another modality for covering the value of interest paid in advance, so that the entire financial operation could be **zero cost** for the state or may bring in additional income. For the economy this will create a healthier monetary foundation;
- a secondary capital market will thus be gradually established, being of vital importance for large privatization, by rallying resources not tapped so far;
- the involvement of both the Private Ownership Fund and the State Ownership Fund in this large financial operation will provide them with significant stock market experience;
- the right of the Private Ownership Fund to charge a commission of, let's say, 3% (which considering the certificate of ownership value of 160,000 lei will mean around 5,000 lei) for the conversion of certificates of ownership into shares or other financial operations, will be the first step for setting up its own social capital. (Taking into account that there are approximately 15.5 million certificate of ownership holders, the aggregate commission, from this operation only, will be 77 billion lei.)

It is also worth mentioning the fact that all figures mentioned above are used for illustrative purposes only, that any percentage can and should be corrected and that the entire process is dependent on the analysis of the real state of affairs. In addition, modifications should be made in order to increase the reliability of this operation by setting guarantees for long term bonds through the establishment of collateral represented by gold reserves or agreements with international financial institutions, large commercial banks, etc.

# V

## A BRIEF SECTIONAL APPROACH DESIGNED TO SPUR THE PRIVATIZATION PROCESS

### A. AGRICULTURE, AS A STARTING POINT FOR A SUCCESSFUL TRANSITION FOR PRIVATIZATION

A retrospective approach is the most suitable guide to understanding the success or failure of economic activities. Before the Industrial Revolution, agriculture was the primary economic activity, being the only sector capable of yielding a significantly larger amount of products than the resources needed for obtaining them. All other economic activities were considered at that time "sterile" (see the Physiocratic economic theory). Manufacturing, although it brought us a step closer to an independent industry, was viewed then as an extension of agricultural activity. Resorting to agriculture as its main source of raw material, manufacturing was judged not as an economic activity in competition with agriculture, but as a mere improvement of the latter.

A new stage emerged with the onset of the Industrial Revolution and its considerably faster pace of development, regardless of weather conditions and benefiting from the abundance of raw materials brought about by the process of colonization. Huge advances in production technologies, combined with an expanding domestic and foreign market, completely changed the importance of these two basic sectors of any national economy at that time. Agriculture took a secondary place, in spite of the fact that its importance in satisfying human needs increased as urban centers developed, demands diversified, and the international market expanded. The entire process, accompanied by inevitable frictions caused by this development, powerfully spurred commercial and transportation activities, as well as fueling the emergence of new and technologically more sophisticated economic branches. Scientific research and education – a by-product at that time of the Industrial Revolution – accelerated the improvement of living conditions in large geographic areas.

Given the fundamental role played by agriculture in the development of mankind, it is difficult to fathom its obvious decline in the so-called "communist system" whose main goal was to satisfy everybody according to "his needs." It was said that agriculture played within this system the part of a "step child," committed to punish his parents for their neglect.

A large number of complex reasons caused the collapse of agriculture during the communist regime, starting with the alienation of the right of property, previously an indisputable right for any farmer, and ending with legislation against any economic reason and therefore contrary to the interests of peasantry.

It comes as no surprise that ever since the Middle Ages there was a continuous conflict between urban development and the propensity for independence of the rural world. But it is difficult to find a valid explanation for the fact that an economic and political system which introduced itself as the unique representative of "proletariat power in alliance with the working peasantry" would promote a policy that would lead to a profound break in the relationship between the peasant and his land and thus destroy agriculture as an economic force.

Among all branches of the national economy, agriculture was the most hard hit by "communism," in spite of its basic role in satisfying the fundamental needs of the population. Following the abolition of landlords and the bourgeoisie, small agricultural land owners were viewed as the most "dangerous" enemies of the "system." As a matter of fact, the communist agrarian policy (contrary to what was stated in the official media) was the main obstacle for raising agricultural production, in spite of the increased need to feed a considerably larger urban population. The State used not only economic, but also administrative means to get the harvest, the livestock, and other agricultural products from the peasantry. The negative consequences are so deeply rooted that even after the 1989 revolution the revitalization process is very slow.

Results in all agricultural sub-branches in the post-1989 period, are reflected in relative low productivity, inefficiency in terms of production costs, and an insufficient ability for rationally utilizing new technologies. These results were accompanied by vast areas of eroded farmland and farmer migration to cities, etc. Now, despite the fact that the private sector has a predominant position in agriculture, output remains below market expectations. After 1993, there were some positive results in the private sector in terms of vegetable and livestock output, but the numbers do not match the general needs of the population. This can be explained by the lack of a strategy directed to stimulate competition in the agricultural market and by reducing the gap between rural and urban areas.

In 1992, as official data indicate, agriculture (including fishing and forestry) represented only 18.9% of GDP,* although 33%** of the active population was employed by it. This situation reflects a very low rate of productivity. If we continue our analysis of the *Statistical Yearbook of Romania*, we note that during 1990-1992[†] all agricultural indicators declined significantly.

In 1993, some promising developments in the private sector of agriculture contributed to economic growth. However, as a result of inflation, production costs increased significantly. We cannot assess if the incomes generated by agricultural activities could cover the production cost increases, and what could be the impact on the standard of living of the urban and rural population.

The state, which during communism controlled all agricultural activity, has not adapted to the new requirements of the free market. On the other hand, the distrust and confusion that persist among many farmers endanger economic growth. A superficial researcher might think that privatization in agriculture, at least on the surface, can be achieved relatively easy, especially if we argue that the new small farm owners, who have maintained an entrepreneurial spirit and ownership mentality in spite of the forced collectivization, are accustomed to competition and have a long experience in commerce. Although these statements are valid, some psychological reactions from farm owners cannot be ignored. We have in mind especially the oppressive role of the state, which for decades enacted laws contrary to the interests of the peasantry, causing a lasting feeling of distrust.

The difficulty in privatizing agriculture also arises from the lack of clarity in defining property rights. This was most evident in the Land Fund Law of February 1991 and its subsequent amendments. Similar to the legislation on certificates of ownership, the Land Fund Law fails to define the concept of private property, thus

---

*    *Statistical Yearbook of Romania*, 1993, p. 340.
**   *Ibid.*, p.153.
[†]   *Ibid.*, pp. 447-465.

creating controversies that may further lead to lawsuits. There is thus a potential risk for both material and emotional loss. Chapter II, article 8 does not detail the criteria that establish the property rights of "cooperative members who did not contribute with land to the cooperative as well as other approved persons." Moreover, given the conditions of a real political democracy, it is not clear if all former cooperative members were – in a free way – in agreement with these criteria. As we know, they were forced to place their entire land in these cooperatives and at this moment they are obliged to share it with others who did not contribute at all. We do not know if the owner of the land is able to negotiate from the position of a private owner for his nationalized property. I assume there are answers to such questions – as well as many others.

Unfortunately, the privatization of agricultural cooperative farms is hindered by other significant obstacles, such as their poor financial performance (due to high costs in relation to income,) debts to be inherited by the future buyers, difficulties in recruiting a skilled labor force (because of the migration to cities), an inefficient network for distributing and selling produce, etc.

In our opinion, Romania's transition to a market economy should be primarily done through agricultural revitalization and by rejecting, as much as possible, the artificial maintenance of huge and inefficient industrial enterprises. The largest share of the financial effort must be channeled in this direction. In this context, we have repeatedly stressed the need for a radical restructuring of the budget.

Let us now analyze a little the arable agricultural land from an economic viewpoint.

According to official data for 1992, Romania had an arable area of 9,356,900 hectares, with a rural population on July 1, 1992, of 10,421,623, out of which approximately 3,100,000 were active (rounded figure for 1991). This computes to a share of 3 hectares per active inhabitant. Such a distribution is unacceptable and inefficient. Hence, the reinstatement of properties, although a positive step in bringing justice to people, would not satisfy the needs for agricultural and food products.

The situation changes if the arable land is divided in relation to farmer households or households belonging to members of an agricultural association.* There are approximately 573,000** households. The ratio between the number of households and the arable area indicates a share of approximately 16.3 hectares per homestead. This would mean an appropriate lot size for an acceptable household, but higher than the 10 hectares stipulated in the Land Fund Law. (Undoubtedly, we are presenting a hypothetical situation, as the number of households could be higher if we consider the legal framework for restitution.)

Our remark is an attempt to find a valid solution for voluntary private farmer associations, in spite of their bad reputation in the past, because a modern agricultural technology backs this idea. The private farmer associations could have a future if the state guarantees the private property right and if the general democratic rules are respected when the land owners decide to set up an association. In Western countries, where democratic principles are strictly applied, farmers associations proved to be an excellent form for increasing productivity and the well-being of their members.

Article 1 of the Law on assisting agricultural farmers stipulates that "the state supports agricultural producers through loans and subsidies for interest payment, price guarantees for agricultural products of national importance, specialized technical expertise, and other aid." Under these circumstances, it is of particular importance to precisely formulate commitments related to private associations of the type previously described. A second, more complex question is observing these commitments in the current structure of the budget.

In one of the preceding chapters on the modalities of applying shock therapy, and in which we presented the two components of mixed therapy, we emphasized that the return of property and price liberalization make agriculture – at this stage – the best candidate for shock therapy. This entails a temporary redirection of a large share of budget expenditures from urban to rural areas, with the following positive consequences: the development of a powerful private productive sector of the economy which produces more than it consumes, relies on raw materials and equipment made domestically, redeploys urban personnel made redundant in industry (thus reducing social and political pressures), ensures basic consumption needs,

---

\* Statistical Yearbook of Romania (1993), p. 86 states that a household is a grouping of two or more people, living together, generally related to each other and sharing costs and chores.

\*\* *Ibid.*, p.110.

stimulates exports, helps tourism,* and consolidates the national currency.

This temporary emphasis on agriculture should also be introduced in the credit policy, in granting preferential interest rates for purchasing agricultural tools, seeds, fertilizers, etc. (apparently, such measures have already been taken), in setting a price policy that stimulates the production of agricultural and food products.

These prices should be indexed to the rate of inflation, and perhaps, in some cases, with a share paid in foreign currency instead of paying the full amount in hard currency for imports of agricultural products. Such an arrangement can stimulate domestic producers and be advantageous for the state. Foreign currency obtained thereby could be deposited in a special interest account in a commercial bank, and be used by agricultural producers for purchases of equipment, medication, cars, vacations, etc. Until then, the state can temporarily benefit from these deposits as it wishes. Undoubtedly, there are other modalities for both parties to utilize these funds. The intention was only to stress the usefulness of this financial mechanism. The currency circulating on the market will continue to be the *leu*. Foreign currency will exchange as any commodity, but its transaction will be more directly controlled. With the development of private associations, such an opportunity will probably represent an added attraction.

A different re-examination should take place with regards to budget expenses allotted to the development of residential units in urban areas (where there is a labor surplus) and possibly redirecting these resources to rural areas experiencing a decline in the labor force (with a predominant share of women and elderly). Within the same pattern, the building of new educational and cultural establishments should be directed from cities to villages. Current priority requirements – in the framework described above – also dictate attractive salary raises to those moving to rural areas, as well as preferential mortgage rates.

These changes must be backed by the creation of an adequate infrastructure (highways, telephone, means of transportation, sani-

---

* Romania has a wonderful touristic landscape; high yet accessible mountains, the Black Sea, an ideal place for nautical sports, beaches with fine sand. There also is an appropriate hotel infrastructure. But the ability to attract foreign visitors depends to a large extent on an abundant supply of food that does not have a negative impact on the needs of the local population.

tary installations, etc.), particularly in villages. Such measures will slowly reduce the gap between rural and urban areas and, more importantly, determine a profound change in the mentality of the urban and rural population.

A budget "with an emphasis on villages" can create an agricultural structure similar to and in competition with the American one in terms of technological advances, productivity and cost. A massive program of investments should be directed toward the simultaneous creation of a modern industrial infrastructure to speed up productivity growth (in particular, modern agricultural technology), the development of agricultural biological research and its practical implementation, agricultural education at the level of contemporary requirements, an efficient transportation and communications network linking towns and villages, and a large agricultural industrial complex. A temporary redirection of a very large share of budget expenditures should be paralleled with a differentiated structure of taxation to assist the private agricultural sector.

At this time, as the conditions of a free market already exist, it would be a serious mistake to freeze prices in general and contract prices for agricultural producers in particular, or to set excessive taxes that would kill private initiative. The creation of a set of social protection measures to be efficiently applied in case of drought, natural disasters, etc., should also be taken into consideration.

A financial assistance program in agriculture includes, aside from agricultural production and environmental protection, a rapid revitalization of the other sub-branches, in particular zootechnics and viticulture, which bring significant income. Within this context, we should not overlook incentives for the emergence and development of a service industry in the form of small repair shops, bakeries, etc., as well as expanding education and culture in villages.

The plan for a radical transformation of villages, as an essential element of the transition to a free market, is meant to offer only a general outline that needs further details and improvements and a more precise reckoning. To assess the dollar amount entailed by such a vast program requires a lot of information which we do not have. We should also add that the budget plan, with an emphasis on agriculture, will raise important questions regarding many other expenses. This is why it is necessary to establish at this stage a distinct privatization budget aimed at financing privatization with priority given to agriculture and to ensure a social safety net.

Under such circumstances, a real privatization of agriculture can be implemented in a relatively short period of time. This will propel commerce, transportation, the food industry, tourism and will favor the privatization of the entire economy, mapping out the overall development of industry.

Not surprisingly, the mentality entrenched by decades of communist dictatorship oppose the idea of making agriculture, even temporarily, a priority branch of the national economy. Nowadays, however, when technological advances significantly increase agricultural productivity, we should view this segment of the economy with other glasses than at the beginning of the century when agriculture was the most primitive productive branch in the entire world.*

In the United States, for example, approximately 3-4% of the labor force, i.e., approximately 3-4 million farmers, work in agriculture. Although this figure is close to that of Romanian farmers, their output suffices for over 250 million inhabitants and creates a large export surplus. The export of agricultural products in the 1980s accounted for approximately 10% of the total value of US exports of merchandise.

Given very limited external financial resources, it is practically impossible to invest at the same time both for large inefficient, uncompetitive industrial enterprises and for an increasing agricultural production. We should accept temporarily that agriculture is essential for general economic development. This will entail an increase in unemployment if the population active in hopelessly inefficient enterprises would reject the idea of returning to the countryside. Such a return is a complex endeavor and only a significant improvement of the rural areas can bring about this change.

The following set of measures can prevent a dramatic increase of unemployment as mentioned above:

---

* Discussions that I had regarding agriculture as a temporary priority branch met with a skepticism that reminded me of the suspicion that, more than two decades ago, met my book entitled *Education — Production*. (The book was published in Romania and therefore I could not use a correct title which should have been *The Human Capital Theory*.) In those days, those "doubtful" minds, involved in the abstract exercise of raising the national income, could not conceive that only a substantial increase in spending for modern education was capable of bringing the present scientific revolution into the production process. Today this idea is indisputable.

- A very strong and rapid development of the process of industrial restructuring that will make known, among other things, the number of people becoming redundant and thus temporarily requiring a program of social protection. Within this context, exact estimations should point to any differences between the amount needed to subsidize inefficient industries and that required to cover unemployment costs if such industries are eliminated. In our opinion, unemployment expenditures would be significantly smaller: in addition to payroll costs, such companies utilize energy, raw materials, auxiliary materials, etc., which could be reassigned to other sectors of the economy. Also, the cost of providing temporary support (food, lodging, medical assistance, etc.) to this share of the population, until it is reemployed, should be computed and determine what subsidies formerly used for industry will become available for this purpose;
- An advanced vision on the direction of industrial development in terms of international competitiveness and a higher purchasing power of the population and not its pauperization ("Communist" industrialization meant the economy of "standing in line" for the most basic consumer goods);
- The implementation of the set of measures proposed in the previous pages (and which is far from being complete) in order to attract more people to the rural areas and to stimulate agricultural production which should cover the needs of people affected temporarily by the restructuring process;
- An expedient program of social protection for workers made redundant by mass privatization.

## B. SOME TANGENTIAL REMARKS ON INDUSTRY

Our view regarding the position of industry within the national economy should not be misunderstood. The idea that agriculture is the starting point for a successful transition in Romania, does not imply de-industrialization. It merely represents a temporary priority, as part of the general process of development. As mentioned before, industry will maintain its leading role to the degree in which it serves in increasing the purchasing power of the population and not the number of destitutes.

Communist "industrialization," based on an investment policy that ignored the real national interests and the precarious state of the economy after the World War II, wasted significant financial resources. The criterion of economic efficiency played a secondary role or no role at all. It led to water pollution and general environmental degradation, which in many counties has reached astounding proportions (e.g., Maramures, Alba, Hunedoara, Satu Mare, Bacau, etc.). It also led to a considerable consumption of energy, inefficiently used, as well as raw materials (despite the country's very limited resources), and created a "mammoth" Soviet-style industrial complex that now represents the main obstacle in the privatization process.

Given the price distortions in Romania during the communist period, it is difficult to assess correctly its status as an industrialized country. Usually this status was officially supported by the higher share of industry than agriculture in the production of national income. But, as a significant part of the value created in agriculture was transferred to industry through the system of pricing and by using the tax on turnover applied to consumer goods, the real share of the two branches in the national income was distorted, giving a prevalent role to industry.

After the population had been indoctrinated for decades with the illusion that a modern economy had been created, ideas regarding a repositioning of industry in the Romanian economy would be strongly criticized. To advocate an increase – even temporarily – in rural population, while the industrialized Western countries recorded a significant decline in this group in their total population, would also be criticized as a sign of regress for Romania's economy. Such critics, however, know very well that industrialization in the capitalist West was not done merely for the sake of industrialization, but for profits. An increase in profits could only be obtained at that time through higher productivity in industry, and consequently in all the branches of economy, including agriculture. This allowed a considerable reduction in the percentage of the labor force occupied not only in agriculture, but also in industry, and the emergence of a third sector – the service sector – which represents today the main absorbent of the excess labor force and takes a first place in the production of GDP. Moreover, they know that the current level of productivity in the Western economies eliminated the huge gap between the living standard in cities and the so-called "villages," in terms of living conditions, sanitary installations, shopping, etc. For these reasons we call our potential critics to analyze with fairness our proposals and in the context of the entire proposed program.

Our proposal regarding the role of agriculture has a temporary character, while market forces, to the extent that the balance between demand and supply is re-established, will correct any possible excesses. At the same time, the social protection policy will intervene to accommodate the process. During this time, the appearance of villages should radically change, so that cities will become less attractive and thus the existing gap will be gradually reduced. This process has a decisive significance for the success of reform and should be implemented through democratic methods and, as previously emphasized, through financial assistance.

The importance of industry in the contemporary economy has been underscored from the beginning of this sub-chapter and we believe there are no doubts in this respect. What we question is the direction and logistics for the consolidation of the private sector in the economy and for competing on the international market.

For decades Romania believed in the myth of the Soviet model of industrialization. The doctrine of the heavy industry, as translated in Romania and other neighboring countries, represented in essence a forced industrialization done in the same manner as collectivization, but lasting incomparably longer (in fact, endlessly). Hence, it required more sacrifices and led to a continuous decline in the standard of living. Although it was known that Romania had neither the raw materials needed for the development of many industrial branches, nor a skilled labor force in some industrial areas, the official slogan was "everything is possible in communism." This kind of industrialization not only distorted the demographics between the rural and urban population, artificially creating a considerable lack of food products, but made agriculture servile to industry, mainly the armament industry. A balanced development of the economy was sacrificed for ideological considerations, and "preparations against a so-called imperialist attack" came to play a prevailing role.

The transition process taking now place in Romania can re-define the role which industry should play in the current economy; such a determination should be based on the number of computers and the diversification of electronics and not the amount of tons of steel produced. These represent the new criteria of technological superiority. Its *strategy* should be well-tuned to the present global trends in this field: the lowest possible consumption of energy and raw materials, a multi-disciplinary skilled labor force, the highest degree of imagination in management training, incentives for foreign capital. The "Tigers of Asia" proved that a first rank industrialization, capable of driving the entire economy and considerably increasing the purchasing power of the population, can be attained in spite of a lack of raw materials, by merely studying such trends and applying the corresponding solutions.

Some recent data regarding the share of industry as 40% of the GDP and approximately 50% of the budgetary income are not comfortable yet, if "the economy does not have a positive evolution."[*] We agree with the author's judgment as private property in industry at the end of 1992 (that is, 3 years after the reform started) was only 11.7% plus approximately 1.2 % the share of mixed property.[**] Moreover, productivity per branch, if we consider that 35.4% of the active population worked in industry in 1992 and produced only 40 or 44.7% of the total GDP, is far from satisfactory.

We are convinced that, in spite of such results, the existing "brain drain," and the difficulties of the privatization process, there are still in Romania professionals capable of creating a modern industry, provided priorities are set correctly in terms of profitability and international competitiveness.

The following steps are necessary to this end:

- to convert as much as possible the defense industry to satisfy the needs of agriculture and the creation of consumption goods;
- to stop production that cannot be absorbed by the domestic and foreign markets;
- to eliminate inefficient enterprises – the top consumers of energy and raw materials;

---

[*]    Carmen Andrei, "To restructure, but not to change?", *Romania Libera*, February 7, 1994. We believe the author's figures refer to 1993. We emphasize this fact as *Romania's Yearbook* (1993), p. 339, states that the share of industry in the GDP in 1992 was 44.7%.

[**] *Statistical Yearbook of Romania* (1993), p. 478.

- to technologically update the remaining enterprises and redirect the specialization course to compete on the international market;
- to drastically reduce the inflation rate;
- to consolidate the organizational and management system;
- to create new free zones of economic activity;
- to improve the environment.

In parallel, incentives related to salary scales, personnel promotion, etc., are of particular importance. We suggest a model similar to that proposed for farmers (see page 86), namely the institution of hard currency payments for a portion of the salary and bonuses, which would probably bring about a competitive industrial production redirected towards exports.

The current law on foreign investments (No. 35/April 1991) which Romania considers as one of the best by comparison with neighboring countries, offers high incentives for foreign investors. Their reluctance to invest has been previously explained in this book and it is up to Romanian decision makers to draw the necessary conclusions. In this context it is important to mention that the reduced level of direct foreign investments in Romania was not caused by the 1993-1994 economic recession experienced by Western countries, as proved by their significant export of capital to some countries in Latin America and Asia.

Moreover, Romania's past experience demonstrates that irrationally diversified development drains resources and creates companies that cannot compete in the global market. One of the great benefits of GATT for the world economy was that it made many political and economic decision makers realize that national production could become undesirable for international trade. Using the Ricardian theory of comparative advantage in international trade, we should set forth an articulate industrial design to achieve a competitive expansion of foreign trade activity that brings about an increased GNP and not a gratuitous flow of it to other external markets.

Another question that should be answered is that of the pros and cons of foreign trade liberalization, which could endanger many branches of the national economy. In our opinion, its very existence is the big plus of the free market. It can signal in advance which are the most beneficial fields for joint ventures and direct investments of foreign capital in Romania. Hence, the issue of foreign trade liberalization should be accommodated as rationally as possible within the process of mixed therapy.

Romania's agreements of 1993 with such international economic bodies as the European Community and EFTA are of vital importance for its integration in the world economy. Although these agreements will not bear immediate results, they represent a promising "investment" *per se* for the industrial development of this country, provided all companies have a real economic independence, are able to control their foreign exchange resources, and the state does not resort to temporary considerations to control their imports or exports. The long term benefit of such arrangements is, among other things, the fact that over the 10 years integration period (until the end of March, 2002), quotas and tariffs will be adjusted (eliminated, reduced or increased as needed) in favor of the parties to these agreements. For the European Community, the rate of change will be accelerated.

Unfortunately, we shall not dwell on the development of state industrial property, a major issue of the State Ownership Fund and, in broader terms, of large scale privatization. Given its significance, it urgently requires a special study aimed at simplifying its complicated ramifications, eliminating bureaucracy, and disentangling the myriad of political interests that surround it. It is no secret that this is the climate characterizing the slow pace of privatization. The main reason for not approaching this very important problem is our lack of information on the negative impact on the economy of such factors as excessive production capacity, labor surplus, managerial inefficiency, unacceptable costs, etc., which impede our ability to formulate a pertinent verdict.

Moreover, we cannot ignore the fact that a real industrial restructuring, in accord with modern technology and the competitiveness of the international market, can, as previously emphasized, substantially reduce the number of people employed in this branch of the economy. An abrupt personnel reduction that would include several hundred thousand people active in non-competitive industrial branches (such as workers, administrative personnel, management) would result in a terrible economic, social, and political cataclysm. Agriculture, even if living conditions in villages are substantially improved, cannot absorb such a large number of workers. In addition, automation will downsize its own personnel. For this reason we stressed many times the *temporary* position of agriculture as a priority branch of the economy in the transition period in order to satisfy the immediate needs of the population.

Although the redundant labor force resulting from industrial restructuring can only be absorbed over a given period of time, its duration should be shortened as much as possible. This can be accomplished through a broad program of development and diversification of economic activity in both urban and rural areas (as previously mentioned in our proposals on industrial restructuring, and using monetary and financial incentives), retraining of the labor force to accommodate such changes, support for expanding the private sector, and measures to motivate large foreign investment. Along these lines, implementing the agreements made with the European Community gain a particular importance as they cover, in addition to commercial activities (export-import), issues related to the mobility of the labor force, services, capital transfers, etc.*

## C. THE NEED FOR BUDGETARY TRANSPARENCY

We stressed in one of the previous chapters that the population, not the state, should be the main beneficiary of the privatization process in the transition period which, undoubtedly, involves sacrifices. What are the practical means for reaching this target? Will the state cooperate? This would be the ideal scenario, but as any ideal, it may be unattainable. Further, replacing an obsolete state machinery with people capable of change and backed by law can produce results. This may surprise the public opinion in Romania. Here are some measures which should be implemented to achieve this goal:

a) Use legal, economic, financial or social (not to mention political) methods to block the state not only from strengthening its ownership rights, but to abolish them;

---

* The issues discussed in the previous sub-chapter, and throughout the entire study, have such a complex and vast character that each of them deserves a separate analysis. For this reason, in the Foreword to this book, the author emphasizes that it is not his intention to exhaust this topic. We attempt to use the data at our disposal (relatively limited, residing in the United States) to outline a feasible scenario for accelerating privatization, and possibly to offer a more efficient alternative to be used during the transition to a market economy. Keeping in mind that only timid steps have been taken in Romania in this direction, we believe that it is not too late to implement the proposed corrections.

b) Prevent the former nomenclature, the elite of the past, to benefit from privatization as they took advantage of nationalization;

c) Utilize the privatization of the economy to create supplementary financial resources channeled in the following directions:

- reinstate agriculture as a primary economic branch during the transition period;
- technologically upgrade industrial production to satisfy the immediate consumption needs of the population, to create a sound and diversified export foundation of both goods and services, and to attract foreign investors;
- strengthen the national currency by combining the means described above with a strict observance of financial discipline both in the public and private sectors;
- secure a social safety net in order to guarantee all citizens decent living conditions in case of undesirable, but inevitable economic and social hardships that have to be faced during the transition period.

If these measures are to become the priority objectives of various development stages and, in particular of the present time, they should be correctly mirrored by the main instrument for programming the transition process, namely the budget.

An analysis of Law No. 21 of May 6, 1993 on the state budget for 1993 shows that these main directions, included (some of them) in one way or the other, are lost in a multitude of other objectives of higher or lesser significance. Its present format does not reflect the very purpose that should have guided its elaboration.

Our attempt to construct the budget, as made in the following pages, is dissimilar to the Budget Law No. 21 (although it necessarily includes its component elements) and therefore presents a different budgetary structure. Its new proposed structure ensures its transparency, showing that our main objective is to complete the privatization process. As a result, the budget which we propose does not have eminently a state character (contrary to the Parliament-approved version). It is a budget in which the state is only one of the players – the most important one, for the time being – in the general process of privatization.

In a free market economy, an unjustified state intervention in the economy is unacceptable, but its influence, through the budget, can have a significant impact on the activity of economic agents (which form the market) and the population in general. In Romania, a market of this type is just emerging. For the time being, the largest share of economic activity is controlled by the State Ownership Fund and the Private Ownership Funds. The private sector is brought to life in spite of some unfavorable conditions. As a result, and considering these special circumstances, a *special* budget, corresponding to this stage of development, is needed. Its main characteristics are outlined in Addendum 2.

Such a budget would consist of a cumulative balance (avoiding double entries certainly), represented by several budgetary accounts, namely:

1. the state budget for defense, public order, education, culture, justice and other areas provided in Paragraph 1, Article 1, Law No. 21;
2. the budget of the National Agency for Privatization, aimed at activities exclusively related to the privatization process, such as:
   - the conversion and subsequent privatization of the defense industry (within acceptable limits for the national defense);
   - the repositioning of agriculture, in the framework of private property, as an essential branch of the transition period;
   - the restructuring, upgrading and privatizing, to the extent possible, of industrial sub-branches (or creating new ones) capable of competing on the global market and sensitive to the trends of the technical and scientific revolution;
   - a powerful support for privatizing the infrastructure (transportation in particular) in order to ensure rapid connections between producers and consumers, along with commerce, services and the diversification of economic activities, etc.

3. the budget for the social safety net;
4. the balance of payments, especially the current account and capital account balances, in order to strengthen the national currency, reduce the budget deficit and create a convertible currency as essential prerequisites of a market economy;
5. the budget for social security, independent of the privatization process, and methods for linking it with this process through available pension funds.

These different budget accounts – which in fact constitute an *aggregate national budget* – independent of their different structures, show a close organic link that allows their cohesion within a unitary system which includes all <u>expenditures</u> and all <u>resources</u> that can be enlisted to reach the desired socio-economic balance. (The budget deficit is important not so much in terms of its size, but in its role as a stimulant for economic growth. A reasonably sized budgetary deficit, resulting from productive investments made under conditions of low inflation and positive interest rates, mirror the trust of the population in the financial policy of the state.)

Our presentation of an aggregate national budget or a consolidated national budge clearly demonstrates that our approach is not made merely in relation to expenditures and revenue, classified in chapters, subchapters, etc., although we must keep in mind this division. Our concern is to reveal for each budget component its priorities and the costs involved in attaining the proposed outcome.

The credibility of this type of budget, aside from the transparency it allows, is dependent on the correctness regarding the forecasts of main indicators at the macroeconomic level, a realistic leu–dollar exchange rate, a pragmatic estimation of social protection costs required for maintaining a decent standard of living, etc. A budget conceived in this manner would direct the monetary flow towards two intercommunicating channels:

a) the usual channel currently utilized by revenue and expenditures, as provided by Law No. 21/1993, complemented by corrective measures related to the elimination of financial elements directly involved in the privatization process;
b) a special channel meant to ensure the shortest possible transition period.

Given their objectives (both strategic and tactical) and independent of all interference (which in many cases will be unavoidable), the difference between the two channels will be that in the first channel the monetary instruments (to the extent they are needed) will function through the National Bank pipes; the second channel will utilize independent commercial banks which should act as partners of the National Bank and not be subordinated to it.

Hence, as a result of the privatization process, the money transferred to the State Ownership Fund and the Private Ownership Funds will no longer be controlled by these institutions and will be deposited in commercial and savings banks used by the privatized enterprises. In turn, these banks will use the funds partly to cover privatization-related costs, and partly for granting credits or financing private small- and medium-sized companies (giving priority to agriculture and its adjacent branches) and to other primary objectives as already mentioned. Overseeing bodies in the National Bank, the Ministry of Finance or other agencies involved in this enterprise will assess the activity of commercial banks during the transition period, in relation to their support of small- and medium-sized companies in the private sector. They will impose heavy penalties to those undermining this endeavor: commercial banks which ignore their obligations should be penalized when applying for credits from the National Bank, or any other preferential treatment otherwise sanctioned by the Ministry of Finance. Upon reimbursement, commercial banks will use the repaid privatization loans, minus expenses, to:

a) secure the balance for the social safety net which costs could not be covered through their budget;
b) temporarily secure the budget for social security;
c) ensure new credits and finance with lower interest rates for maximum terms of 12-18 months for the private sector (mainly agriculture);
d) to grant additional credits to the same private companies, but only when they can demonstrate they are not self-sufficient. Companies should not be granted this type of credits more than 2 or 3 times, after which they should resort to regular credits.

According to our proposal, the National Agency for Privatization (or the General Privatization Committee as we called it) which, similar to the State Ownership Fund and the Private Ownership Fund, has a temporary nature, should cooperate with the Ministry of Finance (which in fact should control it), the Ministry of Agriculture, commercial banks, etc., for securing preferential credits. Upon the reimbursement of all remaining installments, the money from all budget accounts described above can be entirely used to cover the general needs of the population in compliance with the main objectives of a particular stage. Such measures allow an original formula for developing the private sector and ensure social protection measures. They also illustrate the idea at the beginning of this chapter that <u>state ownership rights, once revoked, cannot be transferred back to the state, after the privatization process</u>.

However, this is a political option and the population is the final decision maker. Given the fact that financial elements such as those related to the National Agency for Privatization are not clearly defined in the Budget Law of 1993, the author is unable to make a budget analysis consistent with the proposals he advances. Consequently, it is difficult to draw a correct conclusion if the current priorities in Romania are defined in a well-suited manner in this important legal document. An attempt to analyze the funds allotted to agriculture in relation to the other branches of the national economy would be very risky, given the significant differences between the budget program approved by the Parliament on May 6, 1993 and the preliminary released budget figures for that year.

We have marginally tackled the issue of the state budget deficit, which, even though an important element, has only a limited impact on economic growth in developed countries. Under normal conditions, this is determined mostly by the level of interest paid by the state on its debt and its maturities rather than the total amount of debt, as it influences the general level of interest rate in the economy. This, however, is not true in Romania's case because of the existing high inflation rate and the subsidies to unprofitable areas of the industry. In compliance with the Budget Law of 1993 (Article 22), the deficit should be covered through treasury bonds issued by the National Bank, in addition to the financial assistance of the IMF and the World Bank. The question remains whether the National Bank has the ability to issue these treasury bonds without increasing the money supply.

In this context, budgetary discipline in particular and financial discipline in general, should become the focus of the entire reform process. The prerequisites of this process are a higher independence and reliability of the banking system, designed to reduce bureaucracy and show efficiency and flexibility in the distribution of resources, and, as an issue of major importance, the elimination of any negotiations for debt cancellation and preferential credits for unprofitable state companies. Unfortunately, the current budget deficit can be self-generating due to an increase of the volume of delayed payments among the state companies, an overdue credit balance with the National Bank, and the need to reinvest in such companies if they are to be maintained. Moreover, we should not neglect to stress that at a time when companies just emerge as independent economic entities, the State Ownership Fund continues to have a high stake in the economy and therefore the state must play the role of the guarantor of the last resort for the companies it owns.

An important way for influencing the budget deficit is the policy of taxation promoted by the state. Taxes represent undoubtedly the main resource for covering budget expenditures. Their structure, however, goes beyond strictly financial considerations and embraces vital political, economic, and social interests. What are the strategic interests set forth by a tax policy in a democratic state in a period of transition to a market economy?

a) An active participation of the entire population in the general financial effort of the country, for satisfying vital interests as formulated by Law No. 21/1993;

b) A differentiation in the participation process in agreement with the level of income, as well as the source of income, taking also into account the geographical area and the importance of the sector or sub-sector of activity.

   Such an approach would allow the state to influence more or less the territorial distribution of labor force and capital investments, and to establish the directions of development for various sectors of the economy, in compliance with its strategic interests;

c) Taxes should also be combined with incentives in order to encourage investors rather than dampen their enthusiasm;

d) Taxes should be progressive and discourage fiscal evasion by avoiding to the extent possible the <u>double
taxation</u> (e.g., company profits and shareholders'
dividends) when part of the profit is distributed as
dividend;

e) Minimum and low income groups should be exempt
from taxes, otherwise the state will receive an income
that will have to be returned in a different form. Negative real incomes – such as the interest received for
deposits in commercial or saving banks which is lower
that the rate of inflation – should also be exempt from
taxes;

f) Taxes are also unprofitable when the revenue thus
obtained is lower than the money spent to collect them
(collection personnel, material and administrative costs,
etc.) A cost/profit analysis of any type of tax is a pre-
requisite of its application;

g) Particular attention should be focused on tax incentives
for foreign investors. Such incentives should take into
account the strategic direction selected for economic
development, with an emphasis on the differentiation
between economic branches, as well as conditions
existing in other countries on the one hand, and the
sensitivity of local investors on the other hand.
Incentives should stimulate competition without creating
unjustified privileges, attract joint ventures and contribute to Romania's inclusion in the world economy;

h) As the private sector develops and becomes self-
sufficient, taxes for personal income, and their place in
the entire taxation system, must be gradually reduced.
Such a reduction must satisfy social and political strategic objectives, as detailed further. At the same time, a
decrease of this kind should be related to direct and
indirect taxes paid by the population;

i) In our opinion, the current monetary legislation sanctioning that all economic and financial transaction done on
Romania's territory must be in lei should be reexamined
given the existing rate of inflation and a weak national
currency.

Market economies routinely use their national (in most cases convertible) currency in transactions between economic agents, but there are no restrictions on other currencies calculated at the exchange rate for that particular date. Despite the above-mentioned restriction, in Romania – as in most other ex-communist countries – the U.S. dollar is, in fact, the currency which is used by every entrepreneur and by the entire employed population, to calculate everything from import-export operations to the purchasing power of the average salary. We believe that the state would be much better off if it would permit foreign investors, joint ventures, stock brokers, banks, etc., which use foreign currencies in their transactions to have the option to pay taxes partly or entirely in dollars, and even offer them a discount for advance payments. Thus, the foreign currency reserve could be increased and, if invested immediately, could yield interest in foreign currency. This model can reduce the pressures for creating a foreign currency reserve, and implicitly lead to a stronger national currency. These can be transitory measures, utilized in compliance with the interests of the Ministry of Finance and the Romanian National Bank;

j) Mentioned last, only to emphasize its significance, is the *political* aspect of the tax policy, as pursued and implemented in the future. In other words, this financial instrument should be utilized for the creation and development of the Romanian <u>middle class,</u> directly interested in promoting a free market economy.

The so-called "communism," being a dictatorial regime, was not interested in the creation of a middle class to support its policy. Quite the contrary, the very existence of such a class was against the pyramidal structure of the system – the elite at the peak (nomenclature and the head of the oppression/aggression machinery) and a large mass of subordinates, most of them at or below the poverty level at its base. With the exception of a few intellectuals who risked imprisonment, psychiatric hospitals or the exile, a very thin layer of professionals was in fact under the direct control of the "elite" and had to comply with the "rules of the game" and pay the survival "tribute." The passage to a political democracy requires the creation, without delay, of the appropriate social-economic basis. This can only by achieved through the creation and development of the middle class. The experience of every developed country is proof of this prerequisite. One of the most efficient modalities for attaining this objective is the use of a system of taxation benefiting the rapid establishment of the Romanian middle class, with genuine representatives in Parliament.

Along these lines, the issue of taxes on agricultural workers, craftsmen, traders, etc., which in the past represented the middle class is particularly important. The practical applicability of the system of direct progressive taxation should be re-examined along with the impact of indirect taxes for consolidating the interests of the emerging middle class.

Paragraphs *a* through *j* represent a kind of "Ten Commandments" that should guide the fiscal policy currently being formulated, in order to satisfy the present budget requirements.

Undoubtedly, the issue of the budgetary deficit is not limited to elaborating a tax policy, even though it represents the main source of budget revenue, but entails the clear definition of each component element. The same attention should be given to each element of budgetary expenditures. We witness, for instance, debates on reducing public expenditures, while very little – if anything at all – is done in this respect. Such a situation may be justified by emergency needs (although in one way or another they are usually included in a budgetary reserve), but in most cases it is only a question of satisfying some political goals (sometimes even personal ones), which maintain or increase expenses of this type. The increase, rather than elimination of bureaucracy, the establishment of new "committees and commissions," an elevated level of inflation, etc., act contrary to electoral promises and the rational needs for reducing public expenditures. The negative impact caused by such increases is felt by individuals and the private economic sector alike. Increased public spending widens the state budget deficit, which in turn brings about loans to cover this deficit that trigger higher interest rates. A higher interest means also higher rates for credits needed by entrepreneurs to maintain their competitive edge. Thus, we can say that the private sector is punished for the inability of the public sector to adjust to its real possibilities.

We should not overlook the fact that under the conditions of a free market a country such as Romania, with limited domestic and foreign financial resources, faces a dilemma when it comes to the need to reduce the rate of the budgetary deficit: (1) to cover the deficit by increasing the money supply, and face the negative consequences of such an action, such as inflation, a decreased value of the national currency, a lower living standard, etc., or (2) to resort to credits, utilizing part of the financial resources available in the economy, in which case the state will compete for its economic development with the private sector on the credit market. This would lead to an <u>increase in the interest rate</u>, as the demand for credits is higher than the limited supply of financial resources, as pointed out before. Even if the private sector is still reduced (in terms of its size) in Romania and therefore cannot negotiate from a position of strength on the credit market, it will feel the negative effect of an increased interest rate. This will be the result of both inflationary tendencies and the competition for obtaining credits, among state economic companies, the state itself for its past debts, and the private sector. Hence, in Romania the current <u>direction of the interest rate</u> is probably up rather than down, thus having a bearing on the future economic growth, new investments, etc. This dilemma should be solved through economic rather than monetary-financial means.

A cost-benefit analysis of the existing state companies should determine if the payment for unemployment (see our proposal in the previous sub-chapter) would not be more advantageous than further subsidies for enterprises which are economically unjustified. Consequently, such companies should be restructured as rapidly as possible as part of a program for a future industrial policy, combined with incentives to stimulate food and agricultural production. Thus, new jobs can be created, relieving the pressures resulting from the temporary payment of unemployment benefits. Job creation and retraining programs should be established to employ workers who become redundant through the process of privatization and industrial restructuring. All of these improvements would lead to easier credit requirements from international financial institutions and large commercial banks.

We have not yet tackled the budget deficit in relation to Romania's foreign debt which is growing and could become an important element of concern, given the fact that financial resources are very limited and should be utilized productively. We assume that the largest share of Romania's foreign debt is the result of loans received from international financial organizations (IMF, World Bank, EBRD) and to a lesser extent from commercial banks. Hence, the terms for reimbursement were already negotiated with these institutions.

In our opinion, Romania should be given the same facilities to the ones received by the neighboring countries on different occasions (e.g., the temporary deferment of principal and interest, debt reduction [if possible] and linking the debt to the outstanding loans that Romania had granted to developing countries, in particular Iraq).

Contacts and responsibilities towards these international financial organizations should be perceived realistically. As emphasized in an article in *Business Central Europe* (September, 1993, p. 7), in the period between the beginning of the transition process and September 1993, the IMF granted 8 billion dollars to Eastern Europe and Russia, of which about 2.5 billion was designated for Russia and 1.7 billion for Poland. These amounts are obviously much lower than the amounts needed to cover the costs of the transition period. Thus, the IMF has limited financial resources itself compared with its position to impose strict economic and financial conditions which carry profound social and political consequences.

Therefore, the IMF's strength does not derive from its own financial might, but from its main sponsors, mainly the G-7 (the seven industrialized powers) which use the IMF as an indirect instrument of international financial assistance and control, meant to solve temporary cases of international economic imbalance and to ensure global economic and financial development. By recognizing the creditworthiness of a country, the IMF and the World Bank pave the way for that country's access to the international market of credits and finances, act as guarantors for attracting foreign capital to that country and for promoting trade and favorably solving the issue of foreign loan reimbursement respectively. Given the circumstances of the world recession of the last few years, the IMF and the World Bank have gradually started to show some flexibility in applying its "strict conditionality" principle. This does not imply modifying or renouncing such principles, but rather easing the requirements (what we would call in medicine a "bypass"). This means a temporary and ethical lessening of such principles in order to relieve difficulties, taking into account the unpredictable character of current international events.

Romania should study such "facilities" in perspective and propose to the IMF and the World Bank other kinds of facilities for solving its possible inability to observe prior agreements. Such proposals are debated within committees and interim sessions that include other countries facing a situation similar or close to that in Romania in terms of observing a "strict conditionality" principle. These forums have a democratic character where creative financial proposals can find a receptive audience and thus, favor new measures or adapt existing ones. If accepted, such proposals would add to Romania's prestige and create a more favorable climate of co-operation with these institutions.

## D. THE SOCIAL SAFETY NET, A CARDINAL COMPONENT OF REFORM AND HOW TO FINANCE IT

In economics, a science crystallized about two - two and a half centuries ago, the balance between scarce resources and human needs has always represented a central and unquestioned issue. At its inception, political economy referred to a relatively limited market, in terms of economic agents, transaction volume and geographical area. At that time, market mechanisms interacted constantly and a balance was attained, more or less instantly, thus creating a type of "perfectly" competitive market. The classical liberal school realized that an equilibrium was achieved automatically as demand created supply.

A considerable expansion of the domestic market, caused by the Industrial Revolution, the creation and development of an international market, and by complex economic and financial inter-dependencies brought about by this evolution  produced important shifts in the automatic action of these mechanisms and delays in detecting imbalances and correcting flaws.

This new situation led to the emergence of new schools in economics, that may be grouped, in a very general form, into three categories: (1) the neo-liberal school that essentially agrees with the idea of an equilibrium achieved through a more or less automatic regulation, based on the theory that supply creates its own demand;

(2) the Keynesian liberal school which considers that an equilibrium is achieved by correcting imbalances through limited state intervention with positive impact on the activity of private economic agents; and (3) the Marxist school which believes that only a centralized plan, based on the nationalization of means of production and the abolishment of the private sector, can ensure a macroeconomic equilibrium.

Ignoring the last school, which had disastrous results, it is clear today that the present economic market, given all concurrent conditions, presents many imperfections. Society, however, has tools for correcting them within the system of private property. The nature of such imperfections has various causes, but irrespective of their form, they impact the economic agent, viewed as a human being, not an abstract concept. In our century, correcting the imperfections that have a direct influence on the population has become one of the central issues for any government: namely, social protection.

Due to its significance, social protection has gradually developed as an independent interdisciplinary branch which in a narrow sense deals with economic aspects and in a larger perspective with a new dimension of social policy.

Social protection acquires a <u>fundamental importance</u> in the process of transition from a totalitarian society to a democratic one, and contributes, along with elements previously analyzed, to the success, stagnation, or failure of reform.

Thus far, insufficient attention has been paid to the social protection of the population transferred from a centralized economy (which equally ensured basic social protection needs) to a liberal one (where such needs have to be differentiated, according to the specific needs of the beneficiary). In the ex-communist countries this situation endangered or compromised the reform process, as illustrated in this book. The previous chapters clearly point out that no matter how well-designed the reform process, the population will still be subjected to situations with more or less painful consequences. The impact of such an outcome should be relieved as much as possible to ensure the success of reform, considering that a market economy should secure a higher degree of social protection than in the past.

It is often said that even if the state sells its properties, it remains a potential owner, as it can repurchase them with the money thus obtained. At first sight, such a rationale seems correct. (The author often wondered if this rationale was the basis of the proposals to freely distribute to the population the total national assets as certificates of ownership.) The assumption is that the state created after the 1989 revolution would be identical to the one it replaced. We hope that this will not be the case.

If the process of political democratization is genuine and obsolete structures are abolished, the state emerging from the process of transition should have totally different objectives from the state in the past. One of the methods to verify this transformation is precisely the manner in which the issue of social protection is approached and formulated in cooperation with trade unions and possibly other interested organizations. The money obtained by the state as a result of privatization (deducting the necessary expenses) should be returned to the population through, among other forms, social protection.

From a narrow and strictly economic point of view, during the transition period, social protection should cover in a rational manner, the negative impact of higher inflation and unemployment. Experience shows that inflation is one of the major causes of rising unemployment.

As we comprehend the causes of inflation, we should assail it from different directions. In this sub-chapter we will present modalities of defending social protection against a raising inflation.

When the daily *Romania Libera* (December 18, 1993) published an article stating that inflation in 1993 would reach 450-500%, we considered it an inflammatory assertion, especially since the data did not refer to the year used as a basis of calculation. But after that, we found in the *Statistical Yearbook of Romania* (1993 (p. 391) that the consumption price index (basis 1980=100) increased 310% in 1992 as compared to 1991, and 274% against 1990. Therefore we can assume that the trend is correctly assessed, even if the figure might be inexact.

This conclusion is also confirmed by the data reported by Romania to the IMF.* In this case the basis used for calculating the index is 1990 (which is a more correct statistical approach); in consequence, in October 1993, the average consumption price index was over 363% compared to the average index for the last quarter of 1992.

---

* See *International Financial Statistics*, February 1994, p. 457.

Under these circumstances, an index of 400% seems possible. In the same publication (*IFS*) we find figures for the average salary. Our last data refers to September 1993 and shows that the increase of the average salary as compared with the average for the last quarter of 1992 was only 260%. Although these figures differ from those published by Mr. I Marcovici,[*] as he uses different periods for comparison, the tendencies are the same. We did not found any data in relation to retired persons, but as things happen all over the world, we do not believe that their situation improved.

Returning to the data presented by the *Statistical Yearbook of Romania* (1993), p. 391, which details the general increase in 1992 as compared to 1991, we remark a rise of 342.4% for consumption goods (alcoholic beverages are excluded), which in fact represent the main share of expenditures for the population (approximately 70%). During the same period, an even higher increase was recorded for transportation – about 373% – but its share in total expenditures was only 5%, so the impact is very limited.

The question that remains refers to the degree of ensuring social protection during the privatization process and a high inflation rate due to price liberalization. Put differently, would indexed prices suffice or they should be supplemented by subsidies?

It is true that price hikes were followed by increases in the minimum salary, compensations, etc. (unfortunately the *Statistical Yearbook* does not provide any information).

The local media continues to present the negative effect of the growing gap between price and wages. As this is the most acute problem for the poorest segments of the population, our suggestion is:

1. To calculate the real cost of a "shopping basket" for a decent living, using a list of items accepted for personal consumption and existing on the market at their real prices. Such calculations should be included in the *Statistical Yearbook*;
2. We should compare the figures thus obtained with the minimum salary (including elements related to social protection, but deducting taxes). The difference, if negative, should be corrected not only to ensure a decent

---

[*] See Chapter III, p. 41.

living, but also to prevent negative phenomena that appear in such situation. We have in mind not only political phenomena, which can acquire dramatic dimensions, but also social occurrences (crime, corruption, etc.);

3. The return to the population of the difference (in case this is a negative figure) involves a very difficult operation. This includes localizing those people that should receive benefits, according to such criteria as the level of income, the number of dependent children, the level of basic expenses, etc. This beneficiary list should be updated quarterly, or even more often (depending of inflation), by adding or subtracting those whose incomes no longer justify the receipt of benefits. In consequence, given the current conditions of transition and regional characteristics, we suggest a continuation of a limited type of subsidies for basic goods. Benefits should be determined with caution and granted to those in need, not the entire population. They should be distributed only to those population categories which cannot cover basic costs from their income;

4. Such differences should not be distributed in cash, but as coupons to be used for the purchase of basic items. Such coupons can be nominal and non-transferable to avoid fraud. Moreover, they should have an expiration date and may only be renewed at social protection offices. This will ensure a permanent transparency in terms of their distribution and utilization. As these coupons are a substitute for currency, the enterprises receiving them will be reimbursed for them from the budget designed for social protection.

A correct assessment of the minimum income, eligibility and coupon distribution ensures a supplementary income for the poor, without increasing money supply. At the same time, it assists in indexing incomes in relation to price increases, thus reducing social and political pressures.

The principle of differentiation should also be applied in establishing the rent in residential buildings owned by the state, considering not only square footage, but also amenities, location, real maintenance costs, etc. Within the same building rents may differ in relation to the above criteria, or additional standards deemed necessary.

The issue of covering basic food and consumption needs of the poor also raises the question of ensuring a "material coverage" for the coupons under discussion, so that they can be efficiently utilized. Accordingly, during the difficult transition period, any activity should proceed, as usual, to secure the production process, namely:

- private companies in the food/agricultural sector should be penalized if they discriminate against coupon holders;
- priority should be given to privatization auctions for the transportation network in order to improve links between producers and consumers for basic products for the population;
- the private sector should be given fiscal and monetary assistance for the commerce of food products.

Another important problem related to social protection, in a narrow economic sense, is <u>unemployment</u>. Although present to a large extent even before 1989, unemployment was masked by an anti-economic system of labor organization and salaries.

At the end of October 1993, unemployment rose to 1 million people, that is 9.3%[*] of the labor force as compared to 8.4%[**] in 1992. In July 1994 unemployment rose to 10.6%[***] of the labor force.

The most important increase is structural not cyclical. Among the main causes of the high unemployment rate we should mention the following:

- an excessive production capacity in industrial branches that create products without demand on the domestic or international market;
- the uncompetitive cost of products due to the use of obsolete equipment;
- the lack of domestic or foreign investment for techno-logical upgrades, which creates obstacles to penetrating the foreign market;

---

[*]   *Romania Economic Newsletter*, April-June 1993, p. 5.
[**]  *Statistical Yearbook of Romania*, 1993, p. 169.
[***] *Romania Economic Newsletter*, July-September, 1994, p. 2.

- excessive labor force in urban areas;
- the world recession of 1994, and high international competition.

What is the direction social protection should take in relation to privatization? Without seeking to prioritize, we would like to mention the following the measures: (1) assistance for relocating (in particular from urban to rural areas) those persons made redundant through the process of privatization or industrial restructuring, as well as assistance for the retraining of the labor force; (2) assistance for young people having completed their middle and higher education and temporarily unable to find employment because of the transition period.

We made an attempt to isolate the issue of social protection, in a strict economic sense, related to the process of transition and privatization. We did not deal with the remaining aspects of social protection, which have a more or less permanent character, such as: illness caused by inappropriate conditions at the work place, maternity leave, retired people representing over 25% compared to the active population. This distinction is very important for establishing the financial responsibility regarding the coverage for such expenditures. The budget for social security, and even less so the state budget, should not be burdened with social protection expenditures related to the period of transition, with few exceptions. As such expenses take place during and because of the process of privatization, they should be covered from the funds resulting from the auction of such companies.

Social assistance should be rigorously calculated, either as a percentage of the former salary granted for a limited period of time and eventually renewed (in case of continued unemployment, for a predetermined period) or in terms of ensuring a basic living standard (as detailed in the preceding pages) for those just entering the job market (recent graduates from colleges and universities). The benefits may be additionally differentiated in relation with other sources of income available to these people.

Moreover, the Ministry of Labor and Social Protection should include a department handling unemployment records, sorted according to various criteria (field of activity, age, region, etc.), as well as a department endowed with an adequate system of information and assigned to register and centralize openings around the country. Such availability should be recorded down to the level of each village as the rural areas could become an important source of employment. This will allow the redirection of the unemployed personnel on the job market. Benefits should be limited for a determined period of time and, when an offer for suitable job is rejected, they should cease.

The development of the private sector and its capability to attract a share of the unemployed personnel will gradually relieve the financial pressure on the budget of the General Privatization Committee, as proposed in this study.

Taking into account its limited resources, the budget for social protection should be re-examined, in relation to concrete conditions, to determine if all beneficiaries of state services are still eligible. We have in mind expenses such as transportation costs (in various shapes and forms), training costs, and other social and cultural expenses. Free or low-cost state services for those categories of the population with incomes (from pensions or other sources) that surpass the average salary should be reviewed and reassigned to the poorest groups to cover their needs in the first place.

This is not an egalitarian, populist approach, but a question of social justice, currently practiced in all developed capitalist countries. In consequence, social protection benefits should help not the bureaucracy in this field or the population receiving a decent income, but those living at the poverty limit[*] or close to it (considering the aggregated family income or individual income).

There are other aspects related to labor protection during the transition period which influence the social and political dimension of reform.

We believe that, besides other factors, the insufficient attention paid to the issue of social protection explains the continuing migration of people from villages to urban areas, in spite of the inadequate city conditions and the "brain drain" from Romania to other countries. According to official data, between 1989-1992 (the most recent data available when this book was written), the urban population registered an increase of approximately 800,000[**] with a share of approximately 92% people under 40 years of age. This is a

---

[*] This study does not concern itself with the analysis of the pension system, but the Romanian media shows that this is an area that needs corrections, not only in terms of its level, but also a differentiation as proposed above.

[**] *Statistical Yearbook of Romania*, 1993, pp. 140-141.

considerable pressure on the urban population that has to ensure an increased food supply (even if some still receive food supplies from the countryside), more residential units, jobs, transportation, schools, etc. Part of this migration did not stop in urban areas, but went further to other countries.

Between 1989 and 1992, over 213,600* people emigrated, with a share of 151,000 – 70% – people under 40 years of age. This "brain drain" is a dangerous phenomena. It should be viewed in the context of a study published by the Center Studies and Research for Youth, which shows that 52.6% of the young people want to emigrate (out of which 32.3% only temporarily).** This situation points to the urgent need for social protection measures to stop this negative trend.

Economic training for the entire population, brain-washed for decades by hostility toward private enterprise and democracy, could play an important role. Such a mentality, directly or indirectly, favors the expansion of corruption, blocks the development of the private sector, stops foreign investors, gratifies "well-connected" private producers, feeds fiscal evasion, endangers the value of national currency, scorns the law, the entire legal system, and the integrity of honest politicians.

Another aspect of the issue of social protection is that of the relationship between the active population – approximately 10,785,800 people in 1992 – and the rest. In 1992, a very superficial evaluation, using the lowest limits, shows that the number of students, not including university students, was around 4.3 million; children under 7 years of age, almost 3 million; and retired people (over age 60), about 3.7 million.*** To these figures we should add about 1 million unemployed persons. In consequence, over 12 million people are supported by 10.8 million. This represents a very high burden that can only be solved with adequate social protection measures. We mention this aspect in order to emphasize again the significance of mixed therapy in formulating a successful strategy for transition.

---

\*     *Statistical Yearbook of Romania*, 1993, p. 143. This number only refers to legal emigration and is undoubtedly smaller because it does not include illegal emigration.
\*\*    *Romania Libera*, February 7, 1994.
\*\*\*  *Statistical Yearbook of Romania*, 1993, pp. 96, 98, 259.

# CONCLUSIONS

The reader who has been patient enough to complete this study has by now certainly realized that our model for accelerating privatization differs from the government program in its overall design, direction, main objectives and measures envisioned for its implementation.

This model was presented as early as 1990 and was later reviewed in the book published by the author in Romania, in 1994. In a very concise form its main features are:

FROM A FINANCIAL POINT OF VIEW:

a) The immediate conversion of certificates of ownership into shares and their transfer to those who are eligible. Upon receipt, such persons must have the right to <u>dispose</u> of them as they wish (keep or sell them on the free market, etc.). Simultaneously, <u>options</u> should be introduced in which shareholders would be offered multiple benefits. This would stimulate the emergence of a real secondary capital market able to absorb an excessive amount of cash and to encourage the general economic development;

b) The immediate conversion of the Private Ownership Fund into a genuine private institution, independent of the state and completely involved in stock market activity.

FROM A SOCIAL AND ECONOMIC POINT OF VIEW:

a) A clear definition of the "ownership right" concept;

b) An economic policy shift towards agriculture, as a temporary priority branch of the economy able to compete with the American one.* This purpose requires the establishment of a national budget

---

\* It is worth mention that our proposal for upgrading the status of agriculture should have been taken more seriously in Romania if we keep in mind some new trends appearing even in the U.S. economy. (Of course, the reasons are very different.) According to a study prepared by Calvin Beale, a demographer with the U.S. Department of Agriculture and Kenneth M. Johnson, a sociologist at Loyola University in Chicago, 50% of farm-based counties have seen a population increase in the 1990s. According to the same study, 1.6 million people moved to rural areas from cities and suburbs from 1990 to 1995. On September 23, 1996, the *New York Times* published a lengthy article on this subject, entitled "Rural Life Gains New Appeal, Turning Back a Long Decline." Young college graduates from cities are moving back to work the family farm or to live there. The rural rebound is linked

dedicated to achieving this goal and capable of allowing the transparency required by the democratic privatization process;
c) An industrial restructuring in compliance with the development of
the world economy, taking into account both the demands of
international competition and an increased standard of living;
d) The use of "mixed therapy" and a special program of social protection.

By shifting the financial resources (derived from privatization) to the private sector (agriculture, in particular, for the time
being) and the social safety net, our program makes it impossible for
the new state to retain its grip on the country and could create a new
climate for democracy and prosperity. A question may be raised: is
this not too late? Our unequivocal answer is NO, for the following
reasons:

a) The delay in approving the mass privatization law reflects the
doubts of the legislative forum regarding the methods of its
implementation and anticipates further difficulties, as well as the
possible corrections. A similar situation is noted in the delay in
signing the draft law on converting the Private Ownership Funds
into financial investment institutions;
b) The almost insignificant rate of the process of privatization for
large industrial companies over the last five years. The *Romania
Economic Newsletter*,[*] states that in 1995 the State Ownership
Fund intends to privatize only 15 large companies (i.e.,
companies employing over 2,000 people and with assets of over
18 billion lei). Between 1990 and March 1995, out of a few
hundred large companies (around 800 units), only 54 were
privatized. Further, the same publication mentions that "it is not
expected that the state companies included in the privatization
plan will be finalized by 1995";
c) The entire scenario may be modified by surprising results in the
1996 elections. The coming elections might see opposition parties
vigorously attacking this law and thus opening the way for

---

to the big jump in the number of small town manufacturing jobs, a stronger farm
economy, large economic diversification, quality of life concerns among baby
boomers (especially those with young children), and the technological advances
that allow many people to do their work wherever they wish. As a result, the price
of land started to go up as well as other property values.

[*] Volume 4, no. 2 (January-March 1995), p. 2.

further modifications or even its replacement, in the event they strengthen their position and win.

Ending with this optimistic note, we would like to conclude this study with a proposal, initially presented at the 20th Annual Congress of the Romanian-American Academy of Arts and Sciences held in Reno, Nevada, in 1995. The core of our proposal includes:

**1.** Setting up an Economic Financial Expertise Group (EFEG) in order to analyze and provide solutions for the macroeconomic problems of the transition period in Romania. The group will be composed of 10-15 experts from the USA, Romania and other countries.

The EFEG must have a strictly apolitical position and total independence in appointing its members, setting a working agenda, conducting research activity, and preparing its recommendations.

At the same time, the EFEG will closely cooperate with the Romanian authorities in order to get accurate statistical data and to provide, at their request, economic and financial studies as well as analysis and consultations at the macroeconomic level, in particular proposals related to Romania's strategy for development, improving its financial and banking system, privatization, monetary and foreign exchange policy, etc.

The EFEG's conclusions should certainly be viewed as having a consultative character. The Romanian authorities can accept, modify (in consensus with the EFEG), or reject its recommendations.

Located in New York, as a non-profit organization, the EFEG will try to evolve as a "think tank" for all parties interested in doing business in Romania.

**2.** In order to protect its independence, the EFEG would rely on financial support (grants, donations, etc.) from international organizations, large industrial corporations, international financial institutions and banks, as well as other institutions interested in conducting business in Romania. In this respect, the American Romanian Enterprise Fund would play an important role.

**3.** For the time being, the EFEG will consider the following as its major directions for research in Romania:
- improving of the institutional and functional framework for the development of a market economy;

- increasing the flexibility of the implementation of privatization;
- promoting a managerial and entrepreneurial spirit in order to support and extend the share of the private sector in the economy;
- effecting a gradual, but major reduction of the state sector in the economy;
- sanctioning the framework necessary for Romania's integration in world economy;
- making a scientific and objective presentation of Romania's economic and financial performance;
- devising a methodology for country risk analysis;

**4.** Proposals for studies, which in our opinion, need immediate consideration:

- to correct the directions and methods for accelerating privatization;
- to introduce monetary convertibility;
- to develop a capital market and diversify banking activities;
- to strengthen social protection measures as a result of an accelerated privatization and using multiple financial channels.

After a delay of 18 months we were informed that this proposal was published in Romania in the newspaper *Economistul*.

# POST-SCRIPTUM

The conclusions of this book were written at the end of August/beginning of September 1996, almost two months before Romania's general and presidential elections. My optimism regarding the winner was – at last – confirmed. The opposition won both elections with a substantial majority and the results were highly appreciated all over the world. My feelings regarding the outcome were justified not only by the completely unsatisfactory economic performance of the former Administration, but especially because of the most appealing program of the new President, Professor Emil Constantinescu, presented to the people as his "Contract with Romania." It was a great satisfaction for me to find that some of the ideas that I advanced in this book and other materials published in the last few years are reflected – in one way or another – in his "Contract." For this reason, a brief presentation of his proposed program will be very useful for the reader.

Regarding agriculture (my core proposal for a country with an outdated industrial structure and very limited financial resources), about 60% of President Constantinescu's "Contract" is concentrated in this area. The program gives a detailed picture how to transform the existing entities into viable family farms, to stimulate the creation of sound association units, and to extend services, as well as fiscal and financial facilities, in the rural counties. The main aim of these measures is to absorb the redundant workforce from cities, to set up an industrial infrastructure according to the local conditions, and to make the entire rural area a more comfortable place to live. Special support is projected for small- and medium-sized companies.

For promoting industrial development, priorities are given to restructure it according to the global trends in this field and the competitiveness of international markets, to fundamentally improve the social safety net, and to seriously prepare for industrial integration with the European Union.

The program gives high priority to assure the transparency of the privatization process in a new institutional framework, to clarify the definition of private property, eliminating the existing loopholes, and to introduce radical changes in fiscal policy in order to accelerate the extension of the private sector in the national economy. Also, the program emphasizes measures to spur the emergence of a real capital and financial market in order to attract domestic and foreign investors. These measures include the right of foreign investors to have proprietorship of the land which they need for their businesses.

The President's "Contract with Romania" is a program which must be achieved in two stages. The first is an "emergency program" for the short-term with a profound social character; the second is a program for restructuring the economy and to set up a real market economy. The unions will be largely involved in its elaboration.

It is praiseworthy of Professor Constantinescu that he stated immediately after his election that he would be ready to resign if some very urgent goals – especially for people in a disadvantageous situation – were not achieved in the 200 days following his inauguration.

What would we like to see from this new Administration? We would like to see the government do the following:
- implement with tenacity its economic program with priority for agriculture;
- change the economic directions and the financial methods used in the past in the privatization process;
- get rid of the existing bureaucratic brakes in terms of legislation, personnel, and culture;
- create for foreign investors a new perception of a stable and growing economy;
- avoid as much as possible setting up new State institutions in this transition period; on the contrary, it is preferable to reduce their number if possible.

In the program, for example, the creation of an Investment Bank is mentioned. This is, of course, very necessary. However, the State doesn't have to do this: what the state must do is create a stimulating environment to induce its birth by the private sector. Also, the program speaks of a new institutional framework to assure the transparency of the privatization process. We hope that in this new framework the private sector and the unions will prevail, not the state.

Perhaps it is my fault, but I didn't find any reference in the "Contract" to the Certificates of Ownership and coupons, the existence of which maintain a potentially inflationary environment. (In this regard, I gave some suggestions in my book.)

It is important to remember that the new Government in Romania represents a coalition of different political parties with –

sometimes – different interests. This could become a problem in the future. Let us hope that the national interest will win out over some narrow-minded political positions.

The overwhelming victory of the opposition in Romania in 1996 marks the end of the post-communist period in this country and reaches the goal of its 1989 revolution to put Romania on a democratic path. If the new Administration is able to energize the people after seven years of frustration and to clean, with a strong broom, the generalized corruption from the top to the bottom, there are many reasons to believe that its program will be accomplished.

December 20, 1996

# ADDENDUM 1

## ECONOMIC SHOCK THERAPY PROGRAM SHOULD BE AMENDED*

As we know, Professor Sachs from Harvard University prepared a blueprint for a shock therapy program for the transition period to take former communist countries from a centrally planned to a free market economy.

The first experiment of his program was applied in Poland almost a year ago and at the beginning of this year, in some countries of the former Soviet empire. Although his shock therapy package is probably carefully designed, according to Western standards, the economic and political results in Poland raise some important questions and are now under revision by the new Polish government. It seems that this very elaborate transplant (to phrase it euphemistically) unleashed such a dangerous rejection that the medicine used for recovery is now deemed of questionable value: will it help or do more harm to the patient? In my opinion, these undesirable results are linked both with the socio-political "conditions" of the body on which the transplant was done and the order of sequences (priorities) of the measures required by this transplant.

Regarding the first, there are some unquantifiable factors acting in the former communist countries which will strongly continue to oppose – for a long period of time – the implementation of the shock therapy. I have in mind at least the following: a) the despotic, totalitarian mentality of some of the new rulers which will push them to impose "necessary" solutions during this transition which are unacceptable for an emerging democratic society and a free market economy; b) the fear, among those interested in promoting democratic changes, in accepting the <u>idea</u> of risk involved in running private enterprises, combined with the existing public opprobrium versus private entrepreneurs and profit-making people; c) the anxious concern regarding the protection of private property after decades of repudiation; and d) the lack of credibility of those in many sectors of the government in terms of their competence to implement necessary reforms.

---

* Article sent for publication to the *New York Times* on January 3, 1992.

Regarding the order of sequences, despite the dramatic shortages in these countries of the most elementary goods and the already skyrocketing inflation, the shock therapy program starts with "price liberalization" – decided not by market forces, which don't exist, but by state enterprises. The idea is that although prices will be initially pushed through the roof, they will gradually come down due to the forces supply and demand, although everybody knows that a competitive environment cannot be created overnight. In the former West Germany, after the Second World War, with a strong entrepreneurial tradition and backed by the Marshall Plan, it took several years to build up a free market economy. Therefore, we speak about a historical process which can be accelerated if a correct interrelation between privatization and price liberalization can be established and it is supported by a large Western economic package. Otherwise, the price which will be paid for a lower rate of inflation is an unacceptable increase in unemployment with profound social consequences and possible political upheavals or apathy (see, for example, the last election in Poland).

To make this transition less painful, my proposal is for a "mixed therapy" which combines shock and gradual methods, framed in "mini" and "maxi" privatization models. I also doubt that giving workers – free of charge – a percentage of the shares issued by the privatized companies could be a real incentive given the economic conditions of these enterprises – most of them inefficient and many of them on the brink of bankruptcy – not to mention the difficulties in assessing their assets. We can find better incentives. In fact, the workers will be tempted to get rid of these "papers," trying to sell them as soon as possible, which can lead to a stock market crash before this institution is set up. Beside its populist goal, this idea, in my opinion, will not stimulate foreign investment which, just as Professor Sachs, I consider to be the most important element in transforming these countries into free market economies.

# ADDENDUM 2

## PROPOSAL FOR A PRIVATIZATION PROGRAM IN ROMANIA IN THE TRANSITION TO A FREE MARKET ECONOMY

It is a great pleasure to be again in Romania and present the opening paper[*] of the seminar on the transition to a market economy and the privatization of state enterprises.

Only ten months ago, when I discussed this issue in Bucharest, many perceived it as a strange and remote objective. My recent readings, however, allow me to say that this topic was widely debated over this period of time and initial steps in this direction have already been made.

This very fact allows me to limit this presentation to a proposal related to the main phases of this process. I do not wish to add comments to any other proposals, although we may approach this topic during the next sessions.

It comes as no secret that privatizing a profoundly unbalanced and bankrupt economy requires immense sacrifices that exceed considerably the current internal resources of Romania.

A main prerequisite during this time is foreign capital participation in rebuilding the Romanian economy. I would like to name just a few reasons for the reluctance of foreign entrepreneurs to invest in Romania, aside from political ones, that have only a transient nature:

a) lack of clarity in the legal definition of private property, such as the possibility to be reclaimed in the future by a different owner, the rules governing it, etc.;

b) lack of reliable statistical economic data, such as the rate of inflation, methods used in evaluating property value for privatization, etc., that assist in making an investment decision;

c) how realistic is the official exchange rate of the national currency; are there incentives for capital and profit repatriation; does the taxation system stimulate investments in Romania?;

---

[*] This paper was presented during the seminar on privatization, which I organized in Bucharest in November 1990 (Intercontinental Hotel) as President of the Romanian-American Chamber of Commerce in New York.

d) how to neutralize the role of bureaucracy and its negative influence on the foreign investor, his freedom to act
and to expand as provided by other markets?

e) does the general privatization program offer guarantees
that the government is committed to the process of
transition to market economy?

I hope this seminar will contribute credible answers to such
questions.

At this time, I would like to refer to the last question relevant
to the general privatization program, by presenting for debate a
personal proposal. Please accept my apologies if my lack of information makes me come forth with suggestions that have already been
debated or introduced.

Methodologically, privatization raises two fundamental problems, namely: first, what do we start with in this complex process
and second, where do we start from?

In the first case, I am afraid we do not have many choices. We
have to start with the ABC's of the free market economy, totally
ignored in the past. Its main element is price, created in relation to
supply and demand and influenced, but not sanctioned by monetary,
financial or budgetary mechanisms as well as credit, customs and
exchange rate policies.

Without belittling the difficulties associated with this issue, the
experience of other countries, such as Germany after the Second
World War, shows that the intelligent use of these mechanisms can,
in addition to restoring, in a relatively short period of time, the
mechanisms of the free market economy, contribute to its prosperity.

A new element appears, however, in case of the centralized,
totalitarian economies that emerged after the Second World War,
where practically all the assets were nationalized, namely privatization. This is a fundamental element for raising production and
productivity in the future, as it sorts out the particular order in
which the measures needed for restoring the free market economy
are needed.

The issue concerning where we start in the privatization
process is more complex, as it refers to the directions, forms and
terms needed for the optimal evolution of this process.

Let us discuss the question of terms, more precisely the shock
therapy and the gradual therapy. I do not believe there is an *a priori*

answer to either selection. It can only be determined by the general political and economic conditions of various segments of the national economy. In this context, before proceeding to the presentation of my proposal, I would like to mention just a few aspects related to privatization and the shock therapy.

From the beginning it should be underlined that privatization is, in essence, the conversion of state property into private property. I do not know which share of national assets belong to *régies auto-nomes* (autonomous administrations), but it is obvious that they do not represent a form of privatization.

If such entities fail to perform, but are deemed necessary for the general economy during this period, the consumer – i.e., the population – will cover this loss. In the case of private companies, the loss is covered by the entrepreneur.

We should also underline that price liberalization can only have a desired outcome if it is paralleled by privatization, i.e., the establishment of private property in the economy.

Past attempts to liberalize prices in Yugoslavia and Hungary, and more recently in Poland and the former Soviet Union, failed because of the absence of such privatization.

Hence, an initial conclusion points to the fact that price liberalization and privatization, as shown above, are two sides of the same mechanism, namely, the market economy.

This brings about the question of how to apply shock therapy and gradual therapy? Let us assume that we use shock therapy for price liberalization in a sector of the economy that has not been privatized yet. In this case, prices and, to a great extent, social protection compensation will be determined at the administrative level. Given the insufficient production of consumer goods, such prices will be decreed, as opposed to prices created by supply and demand, which make a substantial difference. Therefore, a balanced relationship between price liberalization and privatization is neces-sary within each segment of the economy.

This also brings us to a second conclusion. To maintain a balanced relationship, the market mechanism and the competition mechanism require that the introduction of shock therapy in price liberalization be accompanied by shock therapy in the privatization process, in a particular field. As a concrete measure, it is necessary to proceed to the sale to the population of state property in those sectors in which price liberalization has been introduced.

At this point, we can draw a <u>third</u> conclusion. Considering the present situation of the Romanian economy, shock therapy cannot include, as in the case of postwar Germany, the entire national economy. In addition, Germany was, at the time, included in the Marshall Plan for Europe.

Consequently, in Romania, shock therapy for price liberalization, as well as privatization, in order to be successful should be limited – for the time being – to the areas linked to the immediate needs of the population. Taking into account the experience of neighboring countries and, for the moment, the limited possibilities to attract foreign capital, I propose the use of <u>mixed therapy</u> that would combine the methods of <u>shock therapy</u> and <u>gradual therapy</u>.

In my opinion, mixed therapy is the best suited for the current conditions, in terms of both price liberalization and privatization. I refer, in particular, to small and medium sized companies, with 500 or less employees in the agricultural field, as well as in the retail and production of consumer goods and the service industry.

At the same time, monetary and banking mechanisms should be utilized to absorb the excess cash and capitalize it towards the production of goods by resorting to incentives and credits or by financing these sectors.

I read in the local media that the savings by the population (deposits at C.E.C. and "under the mattress") are about 300 billion lei. Using the official exchange rate, this means over $8.5 billion. Even if we calculate this figure using the unofficial rate, the amount reaches approximately $3 billion. This is a significant domestic resource for the privatization process, if it is to take place at the level detailed above.

The involvement of the population in this process is the most important element and can only be accomplished through suitable incentives. I have prepared a number of proposals that could be further debated at a round table discussion.

My program provides for applying the gradual therapy to large and very large companies, that will resort to foreign capital to reach this goal. This does not mean that immediate privatization should be precluded – quite the contrary. Advantageous proposals from foreign investors should be taken into consideration. Moreover, even "gradual" therapy should be completed as soon as possible.

I suggest that the revenue resulting from privatization be centralized through the banking system, which could temporarily utilize it for financing credits to additional companies, especially in agriculture, to ensure social protection, etc.

A last conclusion is that, no matter how paradoxical this looks, the passage to a free market economy, independent of the state, can only be implemented through the direct participation of the state. The state should establish over the shortest period of time the legal framework necessary for privatization, proceed to its implementation, enable people to become private entrepreneurs, introduce incentives which promote a smooth transition and thus ensure the general consensus of the population.

Along these lines, a significant role in the successful conclusion of this process could be played by the government team coordinating this process, as well as the confidence and dynamism at all levels of State Administration. The state should rely on the support of trade unions, professional organizations to cooperate with the opposition parties, etc., for the common purpose of setting up a free market economy. The state should get rid of any conservative elements and strive to achieve its self-transformation, becoming an agent for the implementation of economic democracy opposed to its past dictatorship.

What is the outline of the major phases and the duration needed for completing the framework of a market economy?

The first phase I would call a period of research and strategic proposals. During this phase, all the economic, financial, currency data should be gathered in order to allow us to gain a detailed picture and thus be able to decide what are the merits and the demerits of each sector of the economy in the process of privatization, what type of privatization is most suitable, to what extent foreign participation is needed, how to evaluate national assets, etc. Wherever possible, such calculations should be made in dollars. At the end of this first phase, a set of proposals should detail which companies should be included in the privatization process. At the same time, decisions should be made regarding the cessation of unprofitable companies. I have prepared a detailed scheme for the first phase, to be debated during a round table discussion. I assume that the duration of the first phase is approximately 3-4 months, and it can be reduced if some of the measures have already been implemented.

The second phase, which we might call <u>the establishment of a free market mechanism</u>, and which will have to democratically reconcile numerous divergent interests, represents in fact the core of this entire operation. This phase has been divided into two distinct stages, each with a duration of approximately 6-8 months. The duration can be reduced if some of the proposed measures have already been introduced.

The first stage of the second phase will include the legislation meant to ensure the emergence and development of private property as well as safeguards related to its equal status with other forms of property. During this period the following measures have a significant role:

- the elaboration of a national budget with a new structure to facilitate the privatization process and the gradual liberalization of prices, as will be debated during our proposed round table session;
- the restructuring of the monetary, banking and currency system in order to motivate private enterprise, restrict inflationary trends, and withdraw excess cash from the market, without resorting to administrative measures leading to the confiscation of property. These aspects also merit a round table discussion;
- the introduction of <u>payroll checks</u> and incentives for the population to use checks, in which case the balance of such accounts could provide a temporary source of credits. Minimum wages should be updated at given intervals (possibly every 3 months during this time) according to a realistic rate of inflation;
- the <u>partial payment of wages in hard currency</u> for employees in joint ventures or local companies generating hard currency. During this period, banks should be diversified and incentives should be created for the emergence of private banks. (I have prepared a proposal for the creation of a commercial bank, called the "Youth's Bank.")
- <u>resort to foreign credits</u> and in particular to international financial institutions;

- a re-examination of the exchange rate and customs laws in relation to the new objectives of foreign trade, the attraction of foreign capital, free zones (which should be established) and tourism;
- the elaboration of a Code of rights and responsibilities of employers and employees and the participation of the respective trade unions;
- with regards to agriculture, in parallel with the process of privatization and regulations on land and agricultural equipment purchases, economic and financial incentives are needed to support a migration toward villages. This issue also merits a round table discussion.

  In the last analysis, the increase in the number of small agricultural owners, private craftsmen, private transportation, and merchants represents an important outlet for reducing unemployment and stimulating competition among economic agents.
- the elaboration of a separate budget for social protec-tion, aimed at preventing the emergence of social tensions resulting from the process of privatization.

During the first stage of the second phase, it is important that the government prepare economic measures needed in special situations created by privatization and price liberalization. Along these lines, it is valuable to analyze the purchase of food agricultural products on the domestic market with payments made partially in hard currency which would probably result in cheaper prices than those paid for imports and made entirely in hard currency.

The second stage of the second phase involves the privatization of large state companies and increased efforts for attracting massive foreign capital through special incentives such as taxes, capital re-patriation, safeguards, etc.

The main objectives of the second period are:

- to support private banks, both in the capital and the rest of the country;
- to attract the management of banks to the board of directors of companies and vice versa;
- to ban the formation of monopolies and cartels;

- to gradually create a capital market as a result of the emergence of shares and bonds and banking monetary instruments and to re-establish the stock market;
- during this phase it is important to continue price liberalization to reach the level of the world market;
- to abolish the tax on turnover circulation and replace it with the value added tax;
- to enable an <u>independent activity for foreign trade enterprises</u>, ensuring that private foreign trade companies function normally and have only temporarily the obligation to maintain their accounts with the Romanian Bank of Foreign Trade;
- to enhance the control on credits granted by banks, ensuring that they offer guaranties to depositors, shareholders and the state (if a participant); however, such control should be restricted to observing that the legislation is enforced in such operations and not to approve or disapprove them;
- to support the establishment of <u>insurance companies</u> and <u>brokerage houses</u>, through <u>joint ventures</u>, meant to assist in the training of the local staff and to attract foreign capital;
- to raise and constantly adjust the interest on savings and thus make it more attractive for consumers;
- to introduce an <u>accounting system</u> in compliance with international standards and to establish <u>expert accounting offices</u> to serve both local and foreign investors.

The <u>third phase</u> I would call <u>a take-off period</u>. It could last 8-10 months. During this time, as the main mechanisms of the market economy will already be in place, with possible corrections along this process, we could expect a <u>boost</u> in production and productivity, a significant geographical <u>redistribution</u> of the labor force, and possibly, given the existence of <u>genuine competition</u>, a decline in prices and a <u>considerable</u> improvement in <u>unemployment</u> figures.

The following steps will be needed during this stage:

- to re-examine whether <u>subsidies</u> are to be maintained;
- to completely cease the <u>state interference</u> in the management of companies, with the exception of those of national strategic importance;

- to act toward the <u>integration of the Romanian economy in the world economy</u>, intensify efforts for attracting new <u>foreign investments</u>, as well as <u>foreign commercial credits</u>;
- to re-analyze the <u>entire structure of the state administration</u> and to ensure <u>normal conditions</u> for achieving <u>monetary convertibility</u>. I propose a separate discussion on this topic.

I would like to underline that these phases and stages are inter-related and their separation was done only for the purpose of a systematized presentation. Most certainly, in real life these periods will intersect, overlap, without, however, altering the general structure as presented above. As proposed here, the transition process will probably extend for a period of two or two and a half years, but a number of positive results will be apparent even after approximately one or one and a half years.

Transition to a market economy through privatization and price liberalization can be successful if a number of <u>practical principles</u> are observed, such as:

a) All activities and changes should be synchronized in a manner that will ensure the continuation of normal economic activity at both micro- and macroeconomic levels; <u>extraordinary measures</u>, with the exception of extreme cases that could disturb the creation of a free market, should be avoided;

b) The sequence of activity should be done in such a manner as to avoid <u>premature modifications</u> that can influence measures to be taken in the future;

c) Considering that privatization is a complex, difficult process with large implications, the effect of new actions should not be evaluated <u>in terms of their immediate results</u>, generally avoiding spectacular categorization;

d) An economics training of the population through all media available – TV, radio, newspapers and magazines – in order to reject all demagogic slogans on miraculous overnight solutions; also to reduce expectations that the legal and institutional framework of the free market mechanism can <u>automatically</u> solve the complex issues of the transition process. The <u>human element</u> plays a decisive role, in parallel with their introduction.

The economic evolution should eliminate a negative mentality, as promoted in the past about profits and private entrepreneurial spirit, underlining their economic importance. A particular stress should also be placed on the material and professional risk undertaken by the entrepreneur if their economic thinking is flawed.

The mentality created by 40 years of centralized economy, according to which the state is the only beneficiary of profits (which, as we know, have been wasted), while members of the society were sheltered from any risk, but not permitted to make any decisions, led to a disastrous and explosive situation.

The sooner such a mentality is eliminated, the shorter the transition period, and the easier the inherent difficulties.

Finally, I would like to emphasize that many years will be needed to create a sophisticated free market economy. The initial period of 2 - 2 and a half years, as presented in this study, will bring about the necessary framework.

If such a framework is carefully prepared, and the process of political democratization is consolidated, we may be optimistic about the future results.

*About the Author:*

Professor for a long period of time at various graduate schools in Bucharest, DAN GRINDEA has published studies and numerous articles on macroeconomics, in particular on national income and human capital as one of the most important factors, in the present technological era, for raising the gross national product. A resident of the United States since 1975, he served as Senior Vice-President and Chief Economist at one of the large American financial institutions, Republic National Bank of New York, being especially involved in Country Risk Analysis. He produced correct predictions on the credit-worthiness of many countries, the Latin America debt crisis, on the trends of some very important commodities such as gold and oil, as well as in the political field regarding the probability of German reunification, a year before it happened (in 1988), etc.

He was elected a member of different prestigious scientific organizations and has been awarded for his research. Since 1990, he has become interested in the issues of transition from a centralized, planned to a free market economy and has taken an active part in seminars and conferences and has been published extensively in the specialized media. The author focuses on finding a scientific explanation for the failure of shock therapy in most ex-communist countries and for detecting realistic solutions for accelerating privatization. In this context, he presents in this book a critical analysis of the role of agriculture and industry in the transition period, suggests new alternatives for the creation of a secondary capital market and envisions new modalities for expanding the social safety net. The first version of the this book was published in Bucharest in 1994 and received the 1995 Award Book at the 20th Congress of the American-Romanian Academy of Arts and Sciences, held at the Nevada University, in the United States.